THE MARTYRS OF JHARKHAND

THE MARTYRS OF JHARKHAND

Dr. Diwakar Minz

Translated from Hindi to English
by
Mrs Lakshmi Singh (Retd. I.A.S.)

KALPAZ

First Published, 2020

Published by

Kalpaz Publications
C-30, Satyawati Nagar,
Delhi – 110052
Ph.: 011-47034999, 9811692060
www.kalpazpublications.com
E-mail: kalpaz@hotmail.com

Printed at: G. Print Process, Delhi

Cataloging in Publication Data—DK
Courtesy: D.K. Agencies (P) Ltd. <docinfo@dkagencies.com>

Minz, Diwakar, author.
The martyrs of Jharkhand / Dr. Diwakar Minz.
pages cm
ISBN 9789353240745

1. Martyrs—India—Jharkhand—Biography. 2. Tribes--Political activity—India—Jharkhand—History. 3. Jharkhand (India)—History—Autonomy and independence movements. I. Title.

LCC DS485.J4872A2 2019 | DDC 954.127030922 23

Contents

Dedication

Late Iliyas Minz
(Venerable Grandfather)

Whose birth took place in an ordinary farmer's family of village Jhinjri within Mandar block of district Ranchi. He had obtained education till middle level in those days, and thereafter had received training of "Guru" which enabled him to qualify for teaching in Primary schools. But suddenly due to vision defect he could not become a teacher. Bad luck dogged him, and some time later grandmother passed away, leaving behind two sons and daughters. In that year due to drought, cultivation failed. So, in the face of such difficult circumstances, he came to Ranchi town along with his children to work as a labourer. Due to hard work, he could get the job of a fourth grade employee in the Mental Hospital at Kanke. When life stabilised some what, he acquired land, built a house and started a dairy to augment his income so that his children could obtain better education. Resultantly his eldest son could compete in Bihar Civil Service (unreserved) and became the first Adivasi officer in Bihar which was a matter of pride. Actually Grandfather was a struggling and motivating Oraon Adivasi who, by taking part in various social meets and assemblies would enthuse the youth towards education and Adivasi literature so that they would feel proud of their heritage. Hence as per his expectations, this attempt "The martyrs of Jharkhand" book is dedicated to venerable Grandfather in his sacred memory.

Dr. Diwakar Minz

Review

The present book "Martyrs of Jharkhand" is an important chapter in the history of Jharkhand. The learned writer has not only gathered primary information about these martyrs by going to their areas but also collected necessary knowledge from the archives of several States and Commissionaries to establish their actual history. This effort is clearly reflected in the book. The previous writers had termed these incidents as insurrection which had been against Hindus, money lenders, contractors, landlords. But opposing this accepted opinion, the writer has said that this was a revolt against the British rule which he has presented through factual analysis and indepth review along with historical proof. After two decades of Company Govt., for the first time, the tribals stood up in revolt against its wrong revenue policy pertaining to water, forests and land which had hurt the economic, social and religious feelings of the tribals. The writer has effectively revealed the history of the renouncement and sacrifice of these martyrs who have been the victim of anonymity in the freedom struggle. This book is fit to be compiled by all individuals and institutions having interest in the history of tribals or Jharkhand.

Preface

The only aim of presenting the book "Martyrs of Jharkhand" in historical light is to wipe off the erroneous thinking about tribals or adivasis and to reveal the untouched chapter of their valiant deeds. It is also to rouse their self pride so that they would have self-respect which would in turn make them self-dependent, strong enough to widen the road to success even through difficult situations.

No systematic and reliable history has come to light regarding these tribals. With the Company Govt. stepping into Jharkhand, a series of tribal revolts started. Except for smaller revolts, the Vice Chairman of Governor-General Council Charles Metcalfe described some prominent revolts as freedom struggle of the tribals.

In 1831-32 A.D., outstanding martyr Buddhu Bhagat was beheaded, his head being treated as a gift, while Poto Sardar was hanged on 1 January 1938 due to his opposition to acquisition of Kolhan. This hanging was the first in Jharkhand after obtaining special authority. These revolts compelled the English to reflect on the tribals whom they had understood to be uncivilized, wild and stupid. They came to the conclusion that in order to weaken these revolts, the untouched adivasi society must be intruded upon, and the policy of "divide and rule" should be followed. After 80 years of their rule, in 1845, four padres Emillo Scotch, August Bratt, Fredrick Watch and Theodore Jack came to preach Christianity among the tribals. At that time, as agent of the Agency, J. Ounsley was working in the place of Thomas Wilkinson. He had been given the special responsibility of making arrangements for these padres. But despite tireless efforts and various facilities being made available by the British Govt., for 5 years not a single tribal could be converted to Christianity. Tired out, they wrote to Father Gossner that it is not known which ghost and spirit the adivasis worship but they are not going to become Christian. Father Gossner, being anxious, himself came to Jharkhand and obtained detailed account and report. After in-depth consideration, it was decided that whichever tribe one would like to convert to Christianity, one would have to study and understand its social get up and religion. Accordingly present Christianity in that same fashion, and one will attain success. In this way, the padres at first started the work of study and publication which went on smoothly for 40-50 years. Consecutively the British officers and thereafter their supporting Indians also lent a hand in this work. Due to view point being of the ruler, their written work was prejudiced. Hence it was but natural that their study was limited only to the social, religious and anthropological limits which was required by them. In this context they played a double role. On one side before the country and the world the picture of tribals being half civilized, worshippers of ghosts-spirits, wild, murderous, plunderers was painted who had been civilized and made peaceful farmers by the British which earned them high praise, and on the other side the adivasis became filled with inferiority complex, due to which the path of conversion to Christianity became easy. But in this anxiety the "history of Jharkhand" remained totally untouched. J. C. Jha put in his efforts from the historical point of view. Resultantly, Kol insurrection (1962) was published but this revolt was changed to insurrection- the limit which the British Govt. had fixed. This statement does not mean that they are all meaningless. They are sources, they are bases. There is a need to have analytical investigation and comparative study along with micro search to present these books in the right manner. Probably these are the reasons why nowadays the demand for rewriting history is becoming stronger.

The tribals of Jharkhand are naturally freedom lovers. Right from their first habitation up to their life in the Mughal era, they did not endure any kind of subjection. Their Gram Panchayats (village assemblies) used to be aware of all the internal problems of the village and would find out satisfactory solutions for them. The villages would often develop on the basis of clan and the village chief used to be looked upon as greater family chief. In this way, 15-20 villages together would form a "patti" or "parha" and their chief would be manki or parha Raja respectively. "Patti" or "Parha" would be a small federation of villages. The Council-chief of every village would be the ex-officio member of the federation structure. This was a democratic federal union and after the rise of the Raja/ King of Nagpur, the chief of the federation would deposit the subscription on behalf of the federation in the treasury of Nagpur. In the context of tribals this lofty home rule arrangement of so called "half civilized" tribals was the result of ideal political thought. Attention is drawn to the fact that whenever the traditional self-rule arrangement of the tribals has been negated, the tribals have stood up in arms. With one voice it had been echoed by intellectuals, historians, the then news magazines that upon exploitation and torture by landlords, contractors, money lenders etc. the tribals had revolted against them. There is some truth in this statement but it can be emphasized that the original reason for revolt was the breaking-up of the self-rule arrangement.

The tribals of Jharkhand remained protected from Hindus in ancient times and from Muslims of Mughals in medieval times. It had been difficult for the Mughal army to cross valleys, hills and rugged forests. Many soldiers had died on the way. Nagpur was not such an area wherein any subedar (satrap) or Mughal administrator intervened in any manner the internal administration. When for the first time King Durjansaal of Nagpur was arrested, the tribals were unaffected by this incident. Their self-rule continued as before. Although, after the return of Durjansaal, landlords from outside had been settled in Nagpur through invitation and they were in good number, they had yet not become a burden. Undoubtedly these invited landlords had been settled in tribal villages. The tribes had experienced the weight of the presence of these external landlords, but when they found that the musclemen of these landlords drove away the plunderers of the standing crops of the tribals, they started liking them. But the entry of contractors encouraged by the king of Nagpur in 1827 became very cumbersome for the tribals. Till that time the sub-inspector of police, the police and other officials had started collecting four times the dues.

The policies of the Company govt. were against tribal traditions. The landlord could hand over any plot of land within his jurisdiction from one cultivator to another. The feudal British could never think that the owners of small plots of land were the farmers. The British Govt. therefore could not even think of tribal farmers. Within the first decade of the advent of the Company govt. in Chotanagpur area, the voice of revolt started being heard in the Panchpargana valley which climaxed in 1831-32. This was the first revolt which crossed the Tamar valley and reached proper Chhotanagpur, the area of the Oraons. Thereafter it spread also in Palamau. This was the first revolt of which it was said that the Raja was at its root and many govt. officials were secretly siding with the rebels. Some historians have called this revolt the war of independence of the tribals against the British Govt. Some British officers had also termed it as war of independence. The sacrificial hero of this freedom struggle was Budhu Bhagat who was decapitated and his head was sent to camp Pithoria. Such an incident will hardly be available in the pages of any history.

After obtaining the revenue rights of Bihar, the East India Company trod warily at every step. The company had no friend, only enemies were to be seen everywhere. The officials of the company were instructed to behave in such a manner that friends not enemies, would be gained. The power to impose punishment given to its senior officials was lessened. The result of the rebellion of 1831-32 culminated in the setting up of the South Western Frontier Agency for the protection of tribal rights. The highest authority of the Agency was agent Thomas Wilkinson. He had not been vested with the power to punish a criminal even for 14 years. The Company govt. used to advise its officers to impose less punishment. But contrary to this, in 1857 the Company officers had been madly obsessed to execute through hanging.

That Company govt. which had invested a senior officer like Thomas Wilkinson with the demanded power to execute by hanging, exactly 20 years later in 1857 in order to suppress the public revolt of 1857 passed Act. No.XVII empowering the district level officers to punish by hanging due to which officer Simpson of Hazaribagh hanged record number of soldiers of Doranda cantonment even though they had been wounded, physically handicapped and were sick. The Company govt. created a blood soaked history between 1832 and 1857 in Chhotanagpur. In the Chatra maidan of 1857 can be seen graves of many nameless martyrs.

Dr. Diwakar Minz

Acknowledgement

The hypothesis / theory which have been tried to be proved in the present book on the basis of historical evidence had started sprouting during childhood. When there used to be meets and discussions between my venerable father and family members as also important persons regarding ancestors and martyrs, then inquisitiveness arose that correct portrayal has not been done about the Adivasi and Jharkhand martyrs. Resultantly we do not have occasion to feel proud of our history and somewhere this lack retards our self respect due to which our enthusiasm gets buried. A martyr is a martyr. Martyrdom is his only caste and he is venerated by every body in the country. We are forgetting the martyrs especially those nameless martyrs who have given us a free country and a respectable life. Although full efforts have been made that most of the martyrs with their historical background be portrayed in the book, yet some martyrs may have been missed. In the next edition efforts will be made to include them. The usefulness of this book lies in its aim that the present generation will come to know about the sacrifice of their ancestors – they will feel proud and will fashion out a new history by following their ideals.

Full credit goes to my family environment for consolidating my feelings and giving the present direction to my study. I am specially obliged to all the rural adivasis who enthused me through their ballads/ folk songs of bravery. I am also obliged to that intellectual class which had encouraged me. I am obliged to my wife Dr. Delomai Hansda, Prof. of Economics who always cooperates in my writing, I have deep gratitude for Mrs. Laxmi Singh , Retd. I.A.S and former chief ,Secretary of Jharkhand, who died after translating this book from Hindi Version to english and in the end I am very obliged to Kalpaz Publications, New Delhi which published my book.

Dr. Diwakar Minz

Associate Prof. of History, R. U.

Abbreviations

Aug.	-	August
Beng.	-	Bengal
Birsa	-	Birsa Munda Aur Unka Andolan, Dr. Kumar Suresh Singh
C. N.	-	Chhotanagpur
Comm.	-	Commissioner
Cons.	-	Consultation
Cr.	-	Criminal
Dt./dt.	-	Date/date
Des.	-	Despatch
Encl.	-	Enclosure
Fr.	-	Father
Govt.	-	Government
Judl.	-	Judicial
J.A.S.B.	-	Journal of Asiatic Society of Bengal
Jr.	-	Junior
No.	-	Number
Oraon	-	S. C. Roy, The Oraon of Chhotanagpur
O.R.C.	-	S. C. Roy, Oraon Religion and Custom
P.G.	-	Palamau Gazetteer
Progs.	-	Proceedings
R.G.	-	Ranchi Gazetteer
S.G.	-	Singhbhum Gazetteer
S.W.F.A.	-	Southwest Frontier Agency
Secy.	-	Secretary
The Munda	-	S. C. Roy, The Munda and their country
T.B.	-	Tana Bhagat

Background

"Martyr" is an esteemed word. The dead person to whose name this word is attached becomes immortal in the annuals of history. Scholars have not pondered in detail on this important subject and till date a commonly accepted definition of the word "martyr" has not evolved. In different dictionaries the word "martyr" has been described but they are unable to give it a firm identity. In a sketchy way it can be said that a person who sacrifices his life while protecting his country, community or religion is said to be a martyr. In order to uphold the respectability of the word "Martyr", it is necessary to give it a fixed definition otherwise due to deviation it will be commonly used and at every step martyrs will be identified. It has been seen that in any particular country or society, the masses remain ignorant of the definition of Martyr and its limitations. They sumoto develop a standard and whoever is a martyr he is accepted to be revered, whereas the others remain neglected or even straightaway are rejected.

Abraham Lincoln, President of the United States of America, is a proven example. At that time America was assailed with apartheid of black and white. The Americans loathed the Negros and were not ready to accept them as American citizens. Children of the blacks could not sit in schools of the whites. Similarly there used to be separate restaurants for blacks and whites. The blacks could not settle in white localities. Abraham Lincoln was firmly resolved to end this separation which the whites did not like. Resultantly, the whites became his mortal enemies. Due to his firm efforts to free America from the disease of apartheid, Lincoln was assassinated.

Another President of United States of America, John F. Kennedy, was also assassinated due to difference in stand point. He was also in favour of Negros and accepted the co-operation of Negros to be essential for the new evolution of America. Similarly, the assassination of John F. Kennedy took place because of difference in stand point. In other words, it can be said that President Kennedy sacrificed his life for the good of the country. But the American public honored Abraham Lincoln as a martyr of the country.

In the Indian context, the assassinations of Mahatma Gandhi, Indira Gandhi and Rajiv Gandhi had been due to differences in standpoint. Mahatma Gandhi had been exerting for Hindu-Muslim unity and wherever possible used to pressurise the Govt. of India to help Pakistan thinking it to be its younger brother. Nathuram Godse and his colleagues had believed that as long as Gandhi would live he would be appeasing Pakistan and Muslims at the cost of Hindus. Hence, Gandhi was killed.

The assassination of Indira Gnadhi had been due to Gurudwara and Sikh related policy. In this way the sacrifice of Indira Gandhi was due to defence of a special aim. Rajiv Gandhi had been killed because of his policy of opposing Tamils. Hence his death can also be described as a sacrifice. But the people of India have established Mahatma Gandhi as a martyr, inspite of Indira Gandhi and Rajiv Gandhi sacrificing their lives in defence of their policies and they have received honour, too. The maximum variation among the martyrs can be seen in the martyrs of Jharkhand which, although defying the definition of martyr in any way, are yet glorified by the people of Jharkhand as martyrs. Birsa Munda, who is honoured the most and proclaimed as martyr, had not been hanged nor did he fall to any bullet. As per govt. accounts, his death took place in jail due to cholera. Some people believe that Birsa had been murdered through poisoning. Both situations regarding Birsa's death in jail are unable to establish him as a martyr yet Birsa is a martyr. The people of Jharkhand have accepted and honoured him as the most respected martyr. Upon detailed analysis of the circumstances and background of death, conclusion is drawn that alongwith other points, easy acceptance of the concerned population is an essential point which the martyrs of Jharkhand have more than enough.

With Reference to Jharkhand

Among the brave martyrs who gave up their lives in the freedom struggle of India only a few find mention in golden letters in the pages of Indian history but most of them have remained nameless. Among these nameless martyrs the names of some martyrs of Jharkhand come out prominently. Their renunciation and sacrifice have been ignored by historians the same way that the history of Jharkhand and its tribals have been ignored. Remaining in darkness, these tribals are such whose history has not been written and neither their descendants have ever read the heroic stories of their ancestors. It is true that due to lack of material resources, the recording of the history of Jharkhand and its tribals has remained an unconquerable challenge. This is the reason why many of our historical men have been lost in the darkness of anonymity.

The writing of history is an arduous task. This work becomes more difficult at the time of writing the history of a particular tribe whose historical heritage, instead of being found in basic materials that is archaeological remains, is to be found in folk songs, traditions, folktales, hearsay, "legends" etc. They are the natural literature, Veda Purana of the tribal races which means that such facts and thoughts have emanated from evidence of general life and brought to light through the voice of the people. The facts and thoughts remained unrecorded through many generations and through word of mouth as legends were handed down through the generations. These included the dawn of creation, extension of the race, the Asur legends, the victory of the Mundas over the Asurs, heroic stories of Oraon women, etc. These heroic stories and songs have historical importance because they throw light on contemporary life. Sharat Chandra Rai has accepted verbal literature as half-historical proof.[1] It is clear from these that the tribal races living under self-rule were never half-civilised, murderers, dacoits or blood-thirsty as they have been portrayed by European writers.

It is to be considered in the above context that those facts accepted by history scholars as historical facts, being based on archaeological proofs arising out of physical, inert evidence, are today suspect. The revelation of new facts is strengthening the demand of re-writing history. In the circumstances when nowhere are there permanent truths, then hearsay folk literature about Chhotanagpur and its tribes can fill the lack of any written Vedas, Puranas. Apart from this there remains no other choice. If this hearsay literature is reduced to writing, then for the coming generations they will become Veda-Purana the same way that Vedas, Codes, and Puranas had been previously hearsay and later on, after being written down, became living proof. The heroic stories and sacrifices of our historical men are in safe-keeping of folk literature. My duty is to remember the incidents related to the freedom movement of martyrs of Jharkhand which are incorporated in such folk literature.

Actually, the Hinduisation of the king and settling of Hindus on invitation in Chhotanagpur from outside resulted in their occupying the lands of the tribals. Not only this, contractors, moneylenders and Govt. employees also started ousting the tribals from their land. Apart from snatching the means of livelihood of the tribals, various methods of their exploitation emerged. The honour of adivasi women was at stake. When ever the tribes rose up in arms to protect them, they were declared rebels, dacoits or murderers and were crushed by the army.[2]

On 12 August 1765 A.D., Emperor Shah Alam (II) handed over the diwani or revenue rights to the East India Company for Bengal, Bihar and

Orissa. This also included the area of Jharkhand which came under the British. Their touch with this plateau and forest area was nominal and for 6-7 years the Company Govt. was indifferent to it. The East India Company was a commercial company hence to take up the administration of this area was thought to be a losing proposition because at that time there had been no industrial revolution as it is today. The importance of mines and minerals and industries was not perceived and the soil of Jharkhand was not considered fertile. Thus income through land rent was negligible whereas expenditure on governance of this area was many times more. Jharkhand is the country of tribal races and, according to European historians, at that time the tribes were semi-civilised, murderers and dacoits.[3] It was a difficult and expensive task to control them.

Additionally, land rent of this area would possibly boil down to nominal income. It is an irony that today's mineral rich earth and probably the country's richest state was once upon a time a scrub-land, forested, hilly plateau having valleys, which was too poor to pay land rent. So much so that the rent collected from the region was not sufficient to compensate for its administrative costs. Since the East India Company was slowly consolidating its position, it was not possible under those circumstances to pay much attention to Jharkhand.

Captain Jacob Camac was the first powerful British officer who in 1771, established his own man on the seat of Palamau. In 1772 he made Dweepnath Shahi the Raja of Nagpur, the vassal of the Company Govt. and made the Company aware of the military usefulness of the area. Camac wrote to the Patna Council [4] that the Bhonsle Marathas held sway over Orissa and nearby areas and, after looting and plundering, used to return through the cover of these jungles. Hence, Captain Camac took an interest in Chhotanagpur. According to Camac, if the administration of this area was taken over, then this area would work as a protective wall or its entry points could be guarded against the Marathas. This would also open up the route to the south. The Patna council found captain Camac's suggestion to be appropriate and accordingly the administration of Jharkhand came into the hands of the British who, without proper thought, thrust the difficult laws of the plains of Bihar-Bengal on the tribal races. Due to ignorance of legal procedure, lawyer, court, employees and running to Chatra Court, the advasis gradually became the victims of injustice. The traditional tribal patti-parha system of law had always been close by without any discrimination.

It is a point to ponder that with the foot fall of the British in Chhotanagpur, the chain of tribal revolts had started. Apart from small uprisings, the Tamar revolt of 1789 had spread in the whole area of the Mundas which had to be put down by Lt. Cooper with the help of the army. After 1783, the tribal revolts of 1794, 1807-08, 1819-20 and ultimately of 1831-32 which had reached its zenith, had shaken the foundations of the Company Govt. Commenting on the revolt of 1831-32 journalist Jacurie has written that the revolt was not against the Govt. but against zamindars for taking revenge on them for their tyranny.[5] The argument of the authority's side was one sided. These zamindars or their fathers/ grandfathers had been there during the Mughal times and the tribals were also there but there is no information, description or example of any revolt among them. This means that these tribal revolts were against the British system of administration. Still then, the tyranny of the zamindars cannot be denied. In the Mughal times, administration from Patna or Delhi virtually meant collection of rent and there was no interference in the internal administration. As a result, the Mundas and Oraons lived with freedom through their traditional Patti-Parha self-rule and there was no revolt of any kind. This self-rule ended during the British rule and experiencing the pain of slavery the tribals stood up for self-rule. This was an important difference between the administration of the Mughals and the British.

The land-arrangement of Jharkhand has to a good extent influenced the history of the tribal races. The ancestors of the Mundas and Oraons had cleared the vast, unlimited forests and had taken out land for living and pursuing agriculture as much as desirable. Over the times the descendants of one ancestor multiplied in number to such an extent that with them a village got developed. The cultivable lands belonged to the entire village. Everybody cultivated together and the yield used to be divided among the families. Within that a new arrangement got developed that after the harvesting of the crops, generally in the month of May, the village chief, meaning the village head/ Munda used to assemble senior most male members of every family and hand over the boundary portion of the fields to every family. In the month of May in front of all the senior most members of the family, a fistful of earth taken from the boundary land used to be given to the senior most member of a family denoting that the concerned family would till that land and take its harvest till the next May month. The land used to belong to the village. If repeatedly a family cultivated a particular plot of land then gradually that plot used to develop as the private property of the same family. Centuries passed and the patti-parha selected a strong king from amongst themselves.

The king had a majesty. Away from the original subjects, the royal family gradually became Kshatriya and the Brahmina who came into the royal family mesmerised them with the story of Pundarik and completely Hinduised them. The distance between the king and his subjects became very big. The King started settling the Hindus in Nagpur.

After the return of Durjansaal from Delhi in 1628, the royal dynasty was completely changed. Contractors and money lenders started prospering in the tribal valley. They were all settled on the lands of the tribals and were the reason for their exploitation. The awarding of Permanent Settlement right to the zamindars by Lord Cornwallis proved ruinous for the original settlers. As per tribal tradition,the zamindar could not increase the rent of the land holders and so long as the land holder regularly paid his rent he could not be ousted from his land.

The main cause of exploitation was the right given by the Company govt. to the dedicated zamindars to engage forced labour. Apart from this, seven hateful taxes were levied on the tribals.[6] During the time of revolt for every tax a cut mark was made on the body of the enemy. In addition to these taxes, the officer in charge of the police station, the Govt. official, cunning lawyer, they all became symbols of exploitation. After the revolt, the Govt. authorities concluded that due to the land not having a fixed ownership, outsiders were becoming successful in grabbing tribal land.[7] Hence, Sri Das Halder was appointed as the first Special Commissioner so that he would prepare a land register which would incorporate all details regarding land. This was a huge and time taking work but was in the interest of the tribals. Due to many hindrances this work could not gather speed, and the chain of revolts continued.

If the small revolts of Jharkhand are overlooked, then the main revolts which can be considered were the following :-

(a) Local revolt	
(b) Tribal revolt	1831-32
(c) Santhal Hul	1855-56
(d) War of Independence	1857
(e) Birsa movement	1859-1900
(f) Tana Bhagat movement	1914

(a) Local revolt

Local revolts were limited to specific places, and their aim was connected to local work. These revolts were for taking revenge. The Mundas settled in the southern and eastern areas of Ranchi are proof of this. These Mundas were mainly oppressed by the zamindars and contractors and wanted to oust them from their country (Munda country). From 1797 to 1799 the areas of Sonpur, Tamar, Rahe, Banta Hajam and Singhbhum etc. faced upheavals from time to time. between 1807 to 1809 the Mundas were excessively oppressed in which not only the zamindar but also the men of the Raja took part. The revolt of 1819-20 was more widespread and it is named as revolt in the history of Jharkhand.

The local rebellions were mainly against the contractors and zamindars as also against the exploitation and torture perpetrated by the money lenders, and were a demonstration of the collective anger of the Mundas which were however suppressed with the help of the police or army. When the sparks of local rebellions crossed the limits then they used to become a challenge before the Govt. The tribal revolt of 1831-32 was of this nature-it had crossed the boundaries.

(b) Chhotanagpur's Tribal Revolt – 1831-32

The tribal revolt of 1831-32 of Chhotanagpur which historians describe as the first tribal war of independence[8] had begun as a local rebellion when on 11 December 1831 the Mundas of Sonpur had driven off with some animals of contractor Mohammad Ali. The second effort happened on 20 December when a group of 700 Mundas attacked the contractors and burnt their houses. In this way when the Mundas were terrorizing the valley, the spark of this revolt crossed the valley and reached the area of the Oraons. The Oraons who had been undergoing the same torture as the Mundas, stood up in revolt against the British rules. By degrees this revolt received open or hidden patronage of the zamindars. These freedom fighters received the patronage of Maharaja Jaggarnath Shahi. Some govt. employees also gave their help to these freedom fighters. Gauricharan, the "Kanungo" (superintendent of the office of village accounts) posted in Leslieganj office, and Alam Chand, the "seristedar" (superintendent of a vernacular office in Indian court) used to make the Govt. army lose their way in the hills and valleys by giving them wrong information. This resulted in benefitting the freedom fighters and harming the Govt. army. Captain Ningove had caught the deceit of these two employees. Similarly, the wharfinger of Tissa Ghat (Wharf), Chamar Shahi, welcomed the rebels and changing over from the British Govt. joined the freedom fighters and took over their leadership. When the rebels, after passing through the plateau of Nagpur, entered Palamau district, their target was not the zamindars and contractors but to oust the British Govt. Actually in mid-January 1832 the revolt had come across the Munda area to the midst of the Oraons and from here the nature of the revolt gradually changed to freedom from British rule. The Vice

Chairman of the Governor General Council, Charles Metcalfe, had in clea terms called this the war for freedom which wanted to uproot the British Govt. from its soil. [9]

Developed in three phases, this revolt although it had been started by the Mundas to take revenge on local contractor Mohammad Ali, but by the time it reached the land of the Oraons its nature had changed to war of independence and the credit goes to Budhu Bhagat for changing the nature of the revolt to another direction. After the death of Budhu Bhagat on 13 February, 1832, this revolt had become lifeless.

(c) Santhal Hul

Scholars have accepted that Santhals belong to the class of Munda tribe which means that Santhal tribe took its form after separating from Munda tribe. The place of origin of the Oraon and Munda and their migration path to Jharkhand have been discussed in detail by several scholars. Scholars like Smith, Hutton and Dalton have held that the Mundas came to the place Omedanda of Ranchi from Yuwan of China through Mongolia, Kashmir, Rohtas of Bihar, through the valley of Sahar pass and Palamau. From Omedanda one group came to Ranchi and was called Munda. The other group passed through to Shikharbhum (now Hazaribagh) and it came to be called Santhal.

Among the tribes settled in Santhal Pargana, the tribe which came last was the Santhal. This tribe between 1790-1810 came to Santhal Pargana from various areas and after clearing the forest they made the land fit for agriculture. But they could not become the owners of the cleared land the way the Munda and Oraon Bhuihar had become. Actually the zamindar had come earlier and settled in Santhal Pargana and the Santhal came later. These zamindars, through payment of wages, had got the forest under their authority cleared. As a result the Santhals became laborers and the jungles came under the ownership of the zamindars. Very few Santhals had land of their own. They used to eke out a livelihood for their families by working as paid labourers. Their situation was different from that of the farmers of Chhotanagpur.

Compared to the zamindars, the Santhals became victims of exploitation of the moneylenders. When there used to be no work, they had to take loan from the money lenders. Since they did not have any land, they had to mortgage themselves for loan taken. Exploitation continued in this way. At that time the work of laying railway lines was going on in a big way by the Govt. Many Santhals along with wife and children used to work as railway labourers and after earning some money could buy some land.

In addition to the money lenders, the lower Govt. employees and police were also the reason for their oppression. The Santhals did not get justice. All Santhals were angry with the then British rule. It is against this background that the rise of Siddhu and Kanhu took place in the village of Bhagnadih. It is said that one day Siddhu and Kanhu took place in the village of Bhagnadih. It is said that one day Siddhu and Kanhu were sitting with the Santhals and discussing the oppressive circumstances and agreeing that the basic reason was the British Govt. for the same when their chief god Marang Buru appeared before the Santhals and ordered them to set up their own rule (Santhal rule).

By and by the incident of appearance of Marang Buru and asking them to establish Santhal Raj spread all around. On the full moon night of 30 June 1855 an assembly of Santhals was called. About 10,000 Santhals assembled. Apart from other matters, Santhals rule was declared. In this way, "Santhal Rule", "own rule" permeated the Santhal population".

The whole assembly acknowledged Siddhu to be the first Raja of Santhal Kingdom. Similarly, Kanhu's name was approved to become the commander of the army. In addition the appointments of Sabah, Naib and Daroga were declared. Effort was made to set an organized govt.

These people were moving towards Calcutta, killing the zamindars and moneylenders on their way. At first there was no opposition to them at any level. By the end of September some more Santhals joined them. September end saw their rule over the whole of Santhal country. The rebels had their sway from Deoghar to the south-west limits of the area.10 Due to approaching winter and shortage of rations, the rebels had to go without food even for 2-2 days. Some followers were suffering from sickness. This time the British soldiers pursued them and most of the Santhals disappeared in the nearby hills and forests. Kanhu was among them. He had been arrested by the wharfinger of Kunja of the subdivision. Siddhu was also caught. Both brothers were executed by hanging. They had tried to set up their kingdom/rule in Santhal Pargana.

(d) War of Independence, 1857

The war of independence of 1857was a strong programme arranged at an all-India level, but being unorganized and incongruous, all efforts got divided in pieces and it became just a history of martyrs. The soldiers in Jharkhand had also picked up their weaponry and the British officers, leaving their chairs, had taken shelter of a protective place. The soldiers of Hazaribagh cantonment had come out on 30 July and freed the prisoners of both jails.

In the meantime Lt. Graham was ordered to take some foot-soldiers, cavalry and cannon and reach Hazaribagh and to make the soldiers deposit their weaponry. But Lt. Graham was still on the way when news came that the soldiers of Hazaribagh had rebelled. This news had a deep effect on Madho Singh who was in charge of the foot soldiers. Nadir Ali Khan who was in charge of the cannons was also affected. They wanted to reach Doranda cantonment immediately.

The soldiers of Doranda cantonment also rebelled. In addition to Madho Singh, Bhagalpuria Jai Mangal Pandey had a good influence over the soldiers. Actually, the soldiers of Doranda cantonment were divided in three parts, one Madho Singh, two Bhagalpuria Jai Mangal Pandey, and three common soldiers. The soldiers set up Thakur Vishwanath Shahdeo as Chief, and Pandey Ganpat Rai as commander he had once been the Diwan of Maharaja, Nagpur.

An assembly to chalk out future programme was called under the chairmanship of Thakur Vishwanath Shahdeo. The assembly was uncontrolled and the soldiers were indisciplined. Two proposals were brought forth in the assembly. The people on the side of Jaimangal Pandey wanted that the soldiers of all the cantonments which lay on the route be gathered together and after encirching the Calcutta office of the East India Company their officers be taken into captivity.

The second proposal was to join the army of Kuer Singh. After a lot of shouting and tumult, Jaimangal Pandey was persuaded for Kuer Singh.

On 10 Septermber 1857 the soldiers left the Doranda cantonment to go and meet Kuer Singh. Pandey Ganpat Rai had taken the responsibility of porters and ration but he could not carry it out satisfactorily. The freedom fighters were not getting desired cooperation from local traders. The situation was similar in Chatra also. The traders had kept their doors shut and the soldiers were hungry for two days. Thakur Vishwanath Shahdeo was thinking of going to Hatia to bring some money when in the meantime the British army under the captaincy of Major English reached Chatra. His army consisted chiefly of Sikhs. In the morning of 1 October, the British army, which was less in number than the freedom fighters, encircled them, armed with Enfield guns having a range of 900 yards.

The freedom fighters were defeated, some became martyrs, some of the wounded tried to escape to the jungles, and some realizing the inopportunity of that time had left the field earlier. On 2 October, the bodies of 77 soldiers were found in the field. A pit was dug and the bodies of the freedom fighters were buried therein.

Moreover, the Deputy Commissioner of Hazaribagh, Simpson used to pay five rupees per head for catching any wounded or painfully writhing soldier, including invalid ones, and thereafter taking advantage of Act XVII, 1857, would hang them. Within five minutes, the game of immediate case and immediate hanging was being played by Simpson. He had crossed the limits of savagery. These unknown martyrs also have place in the history of Jharkhand. Thakur Vishwanath Shahdeo, Pandey Ganpat Rai and Tikait Umrao Singh were charged of having taken part in the war of independence and hanged. Nilambar and Pitambar of Palamau were also martyrs of this period although they were not connected to army revolt.

(e) Birsa Movement

In the last decade of the 19th century, the religious and political movement of Birsa Munda echoed similarly across the Munda area. Famed for driving away diseases, Birsa sermonized to the gathered Mundas about Birsa religion. Gradually, Birsa religion started taking root among the Mundas. Due to Birsa, the process of connection to Christianity had stopped. The padres of the Church thought Birsa to be enemy number one.

Sardars (leaders) who used to talk about getting the lands of the Mundas returned to them, realized their weak condition, hence they joined the Birsa movement. After the sardars joined him, a sharpness entered the tone of Birsa. He started slogancering for Munda Raj (Rule) and self-rule. According to Birsa the country had two chief enemies the fair-skinned Christians and fair-skinned Govt. officials. Birsa categorised the zamindars, contractors and moneylenders as the third enemy. Birsa was of the opinion that after the exit of Christians and British from the country, Munda Raj would be established and thereafter the third enemy would automatically become alright.

During the Birsa movement, the firing by the soldiers at Sayil-Rakab is a mentionable incident. In order to show less number of Munda casualties, the bodies of some Mundas had been buried in a pit.

At the fag end of his life, Birsa had realized that joining the sardars had been a big mistake. Fighting a political battle with the British was wrong. Birsa thought that with the publicity and spread of Birsa religion, an unlimited strength would by itself come and one day without any objection the British would leave the country and be gone. Among the martyrs of Birsa movement, alongwith Birsa Munda the name of Gaya Munda also finds mention.

(f) Tana Bhagat Movement

From a racial point of view, the Oraon is a special tribe compared to most of the tribes of Jharkhand. This tribe is not of Kol origin, and in the primary period its ancestors had been in touch with the Dravids in south India. Its language is Kurukh which has similarity with Tamil language. During the time of migrating to Chhotanagpur from down south the ancestors of Oraons had stayed in Shahabad. Here they came in contact with the Aryans due to which the level of their social life went up. They were given the equivalent position of Brahmans. After entering Chhotanagpur they came in contact with the Mundas and the level of their social life started going down. Downfall came in the way they started believing in ghosts and spirits, eating vile food, taking off their sacred thread etc. The Tana Bhagat movement is for restoring the ancient kurukh society by freeing the Oraons of the aforementioned vices.

The founder of the Tana Bhagat movement was a 20 years old youth called Jatra Oraon. Dharmes (supreme God of the Oraons) had ordered him that he should direct the Oraons that they should not be afraid of ghosts and spirits, they should not touch meat or wine. He should give instructions to the Oraons that instead of being frightened by ghosts and spirits they should drive them away, they should not kill any creature, they should bathe daily and worship Dharmes. Jatra also told the Oraons that they had received their land from their ancestors therefore they should stop paying land rent. Jatra further said that Oraons should not sell their labour to other races because so long as they would be selling their labour they would remain poor. Jatra was charged for inciting the Oraons and rioting due to which he was punished for one and a half years. It is said that zamindars got him beaten up in jail. Jatra died within a few months after coming out of jail. The death of Jatra was the death of a martyr. The Oraons had stopped working as laborers, due to which the work of the zamindars came to a standstill. Hence they had wanted to cripple Jatra or finish him off. After Jatra, other Bhagat preceptors took over the movement. The Tana Bhagat movement got rejuvenated after getting the patronage of Mahatma Gandhi.

The Tana Bhagat movement was actually a reformist movement. The living habits of the Oraons had descended to a low level. The Mundas themselves had accepted that when the Oraons had entered Chhotanagpur, they had been wearing sacred thread and their social life had been of a high level. The Tana Bhagats wanted to uplift the social and economic standard of life of the Oraons. The Tana Bhagats said that so long as the Oraons worked for others as servants and labourers, they would remain poor.

The Oraons left serving others. The fields of the zamindars and other rich persons remained unploughed. This was a revolutionary step.

For Jharkhand, especially during the period of company rule, it was a period of revolts. During this period the tribals were exploited in many ways. Due to information about tribal revolts and their reason, Jharkhand came under the non-regulation administrative system.

List of Reference books

1. S. C. Roy, The Mundas and their country, Ranchi, Reprint 1995, Pg. 2.
2. J. C. Jha, And when the people rose in protest, they were treated as murderers and hunted down by troops- The Tribal Revolt of Chhotanagpur, (1831-32), Patna, 1987, Pg. 47.
3. L. S. S. O. Malley, History of Bengal, Bihar and Orissa under British Rule, Calcutta, 1925, Pg. 668.
4. Ranchi Gazetteer quotes Camac-whose (Raja Nagpur) country would form an effective barrier to the incursions of the Marathas, thus covering Bihar and Birbhum and at the same time giving them the command of the passes into the Deccan. Pg. 45.
5. Jacqueries, "revolt not against the Govt. but against the zamindars seeking the wild justice of revenge." Calcutta Review, July 1869, Pg. 143.
6. (A) S. C. Roy, The Mundas and their Country, Ranchi, Reprint 1995, Pg. 133 (B) J. C. Jha, The Tribal Revolt of Chhotanagpur (1831-32), Patna 1987, Pg. : 173.
7. Bhuinhari settlement under Bengal Act II of 1869.
8. P. C. Roy Choudhary- It had more right to be regarded as a freedom struggle by the half civilized jungle folks than the movement of 1857, Singhbhum Gazetteer, Patna, 1958, Pg.: 83.
9. Charles Metcalfe..... they did intend to expel the British Govt. from their own country and establish their own independence.... Charles Metcalfe minute, 14 April, 1832, Beng. G.Judl.Cons. no.:17 dth 19 June, 1832, W.B.S.A.
10. District Gazetteer Santhal Parganas- on 10 Sept. the whole country from Deoghar to South-western border of the district was in their hands.... Pg.: 51.

Chapter: One

Historical Mile stone Singi Dei : Jani Shikar

(Even in folk tradition, Sin-gi Dei has an unforgettable place and due to finding mention in folksongs (Jani Shikar), this custom has become for women a high level social symbol of Pride. Sin-gi Dei has the pride of place of being the first martyr in her society).

In the history of the tribals settled in Jharkhand, jani shikar is a singular incident when the Oraon amazons donned men's clothes, and taking the place of men, not only faced the enemy but also drove them off. After leaving Shahabad, the ancestors of the Oraons had taken shelter in the plateau of Rohtasgarh.[1] When they reached Rohtasgarh, they had to face the Kharwars who had settled there before. After gaining victory over the Kharwars, they built a strong fortress on the 1500 feet high plateau of Rohtasgarh for protection from enemies. This they surrounded with a high rampart which completed the protective measures so that it became impenetrable to the enemies.[2] "Sarhul" or "Khaddi" is an ancient and most important festival of the Oraons. In Kurukh language it is famous as "Khekhel Benja" which is celebrated every year in the month of Chait. This not only symbolizes the marriage of the Earth and the Sun through which the increase in fertility of the earth is indicated, but also symbolizes prosperity and merriment.

Alongwith the merriment of the Oraons, intoxicated nature of the month of Chaith passes on the light breeze of its blossoms. During this occasion, song and dance and drinking "hadia" is very common. This is not a matter of present times but centuries ago Sarhul, Khaddi or Khekhel Benja used to be celebrated with rejoicing and merriment. The history and folk tale of Jani Shikar is of an incident of Rohtasgarh.

The Chero tribe was the traditional enemy of the Oraon. This tribe of the Kol race was supposed to be wild, half-civilised and having dietary habits of a low society, dirty, an outcaste race. Compared to the high level of their social status, the Oraons thought the Cheros to be of low level and that they could stoop to any depth or level. According to Buchanan, the Brahmans even today consider the Chero and Kharwar to be outcaste.[3]

Prior to Sarhul, the Cheros had tried to penetrate the Rohtasgarh fort of the Oraons quite a few times, but they could not penetrate the strong fort built at a height. Ultimately, they enticed a milk maid who used to supply milk in the fort and learnt the secret due to which they became successful in their attack.

The milk maid had told them to wait till the festival of Khaddi because on that day all the Oraons remain busy in the festivities. Hence, success could be achieved through a sudden attack. The plan was accordingly prepared. When on the night of Sarhul all the Oraons were intoxicated then the Cheros attacked them.[4] But they were in for a big surprise. Various groups of men with turban on their heads, and bows and arrows as also swords in their hands came to face them and opposed fiercely. It was not possible for the shocked enemies to endure the sudden attack. Somehow they managed to run away. They thought that the milk maid despite taking money had given them false information. Ultimately the milk maid was caught but she said, "I was not wrong, but you were stupid. They were not men but women who had dressed up as men and defeated you. They had been led by a woman named Sin-gi Dei.[5] She was an expert warrior and skilful strategist. She had quickly formed the various groups of the troops and encircling you she defeated you through well organized strategy.

This knowledge hurt the manly pride of the Cheros so they attacked again but yet again they had to face defeat. The troop of Oraon women drove them away across the river. The troops of Sin-gi Dei became exhausted after these two consecutive battles hence on their return they stopped by the river to wash their hands and face in order to refresh themselves. On the other hand the Cheros could not believe whether they were women or men. So in order to find out, some Cheros hid them-selves in bushes near the river bank. Women wash their faces by taking water in both hands and splashing it from the top down wards whereas men take water in one hand and splash it on their face. The spies of the Chero army observed that like women all the Oraon troop members were washing their face and hands and that indeed they were women. On their return they confidently informed that in the Oraon army all were women. Thereafter the Chero army, with greater enthusiasm, prepared for an attack as per a new war strategy and attacked them. There was fierce fighting and every Oraon woman fought to the end and got killed. In the end Sin-gi Dei also died a brave warrior's death in the battle. The Chero army entered the impenetrable fort built by the Oraons. The men were in-toxicated with Sarhul. They were not capable of opposing them. The Chero army drove away the Oraons in that state from Rohtasgarh. After the intoxication ended, the despondent, disheartened and drained out Oraons crossed the Sahar valley[6] and with the help of the north Koel river turned towards Jharkhand.[7]

Oraon women are amazons. During times of trouble and hostile circumstances, they deal with such odds with strength and wisdom. The kurukh folk songs reflect examples of bravery and wisdom of Oraon women. They are much more laborious and brave than the men.[8] In dancing and singing the young women may be participating with young men throughout the night yet they do not become tired. Hence, while living in Rohtasgarh the action taken by the Oraon women army could only be possible by amazons.

Today's "jani shikar" is celebrated in memory of this incident which happened centuries ago in which Oraon women wear men's attire and armed with bows and arrows, swords and traditional weapons come out in groups. Wherever they want, they go for "shikar" or hunt and kill or catch animals and birds symbolizing the enemy. These animals and birds may be wild or domesticated. This celebration in honour of that memory is celebrated after every 12 years. On this occasion, no man stops or comments on this celebration-in fact men welcome them. They arrange for drinking water for them. On this occasion, the whole day belongs to the women. This recalls to mind those brave women warriors who sacrificed their lives trying to protect their society. It enthuses that in future they will again do it. After hunting throughout the day, they assemble in the evening in the village "akhra". They deposit their prey and worship Dharmes, Sun, Earth and Sarna Mother. Thereafter they cook the hunted victims and the food is religiously offered. Series of dances to the tune of folk songs related to Sin-gi Dei and the Oraon women warriors continue till late night. Their wearing of men's attire bring into prominence their Amazonian similarity.

This celebration coming down from thousands of years ago has become so popular and glorified that now jani shikar is celebrated not only by Oraon woman but by other tribal and "Sadan" women. This now gives the appearance of a regional tradition.

There is an interesting fact regarding this occasion as to why it is celebrated with intervals of 12 years. It is known that the kumbh mela is celebrated in four pilgrimage places in an interval of 12 years. As per Sun principle and Hindu Astrological Treatise all the constellations of the universe complete one circumambulation of the Sun within 12 years. Zodiac signs, transit, month and "vritti" are also 12 in number. As described in the Puranas 12 years constitute one "yug".[9] The question arises what connection to 12 years does "jani shikar" of these tribals have-the same tribals who have been described by the British and their supportive writers as uncivilized, bar-barian, looters, killers and worshippers of ghosts and spirits.

On many occasions in newspapers- magazines or seminars it has been commonly mentioned that in Rohtasgarh the Mughals or Turks had attacked the Oraons after learning the secret from the milk maid, and Oraon women after donning men's clothes had faced the onslaught. In Oraon tradition this tale remained alive through hearsay that the "Mlechchas" defeated the Oraons through deception. Later on when Sir Herbert Risley's book "Tribals and castes of Bengal" was published in 1891, he defined the meaning of "Mlechcha" to be "Mughal"[10] and proclaimed that they were Mughals who had ambushed the Oraons.

In this proclamation not only did the British take interest but also the Christian Missionaries who tried to psychologically influence the Oraons against the Muslims, but in the Shahabad gazetteer it has been clearly mentioned that "this is a proven tradition that the governance of Rohtasgarh has consecutively been run by the Kharwar, Oraon and Cheros. The Oraons emphasize on this point that Rohtasgarh was originally under the authority of their leaders. But Hindus through guila attacked and defeated them on the occasion of their national festival, a time when the Oraon men were dead drunk and only women faced their attack.[11]

The only Indian research scholar of British times S. C. Roy agreed with Risley that the word "Mlechcha" denoted Mughal and also agreed with the word Hindu. Analyzing the social and cultural differences between the Oraons of eastern Ranchi and western Ranchi, he has said that the Oraons of eastern Ranchi appear to have come from Rohtasgarh while the Oraons of western Ranchi came to Chhotanagpur probably around the 13th century after having been defeated by the Mughals.[12]

The entry of Oraons into the province of Chhotangpur may be ascertained through 4 reliable sources – (i) Phanimukut Rai of Nagvanshi Kingdom (ii) Ptolemy's Ancient Geography (iii) The Asokan period (271-231 B.C.) Savar race (iv) The Malai or Maler of Megasthenes.

(1) The first king of the Nagvanshi lineage was Phanimukut Rai. He was coronated in Vikram samvat 121 meaning 64 A.D. This date

is mentioned in Veni Sagar Mehta's Nagvanshavali. The Oraons and Mundas had taken part in the coronation ceremony. This proves that the Oraons had been fully established in their political existence. E.T. Dalton has also written about the presence of Mundas and Oraons in this coronation ceremony.[13] Hence in the 3rd century the Oraons had fully settled in Jharkhand.

(2) The second source is based on the statement of Ptolemy which he has quoted in his book Ancient Geography. He has described Chhotanagpur by the name of Kokonagai. He has explained that Kokonagai was settled beside the river Ganga whose capital was Doisa or Dosara.[14] Actually "gai" or the word "gahi" is used as a suffix in Kurukh language. The word means "Kurukh home or country." Actually Ptolemy saw an amplitude of Oraons every where so he named the area as Kokna-gai. In this way, on the basis of Ptolemy's book Ancient Geography, the Oraons had probably entered in the 3rd. century.

(3) During the Mughal times and even earlier, Shahabad district used to be governed by the Kurukhas race. This area was connected to Magadh kingdom.[15] According to Buchanan, Karush, Bhar, three Rajput brothers, Chero (twice) and Savar had connected to Magadh Empire and governed Shahabad. It is not certain regarding the first three rulers, but the Cheros were certainly rulers of this area who were defeated by the Savars during the Asokan period (273-236 B.C.)[16] On the basis of his-torical facts, it has been very well accepted that the Oraons were defeated in Rohtasgarh and fled the place about a century earlier to the Asokan period.

(4) In about 305 B.C., Megasthenes, the Greek ambassador who had come to the Mauryan court, had written a book named Indica which has been recognized as a historical source. In this book he has described the Maler tribe. From various sources it has been proved that the ancestors of the Oraons and the Malers of Rajmahal hills were the same. Megasthenes in his commentary has brought to light that the Malers lived in the area of Parasi which was situated in between Magadha and the lower part of Bengal. This place was surrounded by the Ganga and the Malas hills.[17] Indica clearly describes that the country of the Maler tribe was was situated in the Malas hills which was surrounded by the river Ganga.[18] The historians have identified Malas hills and Mandar hill to be situated south of modern day Bhagalpur and the flow area of the Santhal Pargans Ganga. Which means that in the

last phase of 4th century B.C. the Malai or Maler tribe had already entered Santhal Pargana. This also proves that the ancestors of the Oraons had left Rohtasgarh in the earlier part of 4th century B.C.

This gossip or general belief arose out of the commentary of Risley. It appears that during the time of Risley, the word "Mlechcha" meant Muslim Turk or Mughal and probably due to this reason it was thought that "Malechcha" would mean Mughal. Being influenced by the British, even learned scholarly Oraons slowly started believing the commentary as true. Nobody tried to examine from historical point of view as to when the Oraons had entered Jharkhand.

The fact is that Muslims in the form of Bakhtiyar Khilji entered Bihar in the 12th century, and the history of Rohtasgarh states that prior to 1359 the Muslims had no claim to authority in Rohtasgarh. The proofs of the time of Emperor Asoka (270-23 B.C.) clarify that the Kurukhs after having been defeated by the Cheros, left Rohtasgarh area in 4th century B.C. (Dr. Buchanan, Eastern India, part one, Pg.:406-7). Everyone has accepted the fact of the presence of Oraons in the coronation of Raja Phanimukut Rai, the first Nagvanshi Raja. There are also other historical evidence which reveal that in the period when the Oraon tribe had entered ?Chhotanagpur and got settled there, at that time no one by the name of Mughal had existed there. In this context it would be necessary to consider the note of Hunter on Pg.: 146 of the Shahabad Gazetteer wherein it has been stated that the Oraons settled in the western part of Ranchi are from the cultural viewpoint much more developed than the Oraons who had earlier settled there. It seems that in the 12-13th century the Oraons came to Chhotanagpur from Shahabad in groups. This statement is true that the Oraons had been in sufficient number in Shahabad and they successively came in groups and settled there but at that time they were ordinary citizens. They were neither the ruler nor were their rule set up twice in Rohtasgarh. There is no historical proof that they were attacked there by the Mughals. The misleading incident as proclaimed by Risley and S. C. Roy has no historical basis of its confirmation.

At present, despite the haziness of history, the incident of jani shikar appears to be historical and a milestone from where a new chapter of Oraon life begins. In folklore, it has an unforgettable place and, captured in folk songs, this custom symbolizes to women high level social pride. Be it known that any famous incident finds place in the voice of common people through folksong when it happens quite some time back and the ordinary folk have no suspicion regarding its reliability.

List of Reference books

1. S. C. Roy, the Oraons of Chhotanagpur, Man in India office, Ranchi, 1984, Pg.: 24.
2. L. S. S. O, Malley, Bengal, Bihar and Orissa census Report, 1911, Part-I, Pg: 402, Calcutta, 1906, Pg.:9, 17.
3. Buchanan, Eastern India, Vol.I, Monogonary Marteu, London, 1938, Pg.:405-07.
4. P. C. Roy Choudhary, Bihar District Gazetteers : Shahabad, Govt. of Bihar, Patna, 1966, Pg.:461-68.
5. On the basis of Pahan Conference held on 04/10/98 (Baro) and 5/11/98 (Murma, Ranchi).
6. N. Kumar, Bihar District Gazetteers : Ranchi, Govt. of Bihar, Patna, Pg.: 41.
7. W. W. Hunter, quoted in Shahabad Gazetteer, Pg.: 146
8. P. C. Roy Choudhary, Shahabad Gazetteer, op.cit. Pg.: 147
9. P. V. Kane, History of Dharmashastra, Vol.IV, Bhandarkar Institute, Pune, 1966.
10. H. H. Risley, Tribes and Casts of Bengal, Vol. II, Calcutta, 1891, Pg.: 139
11. P. C. Roy Choudhary, Shahabad Gazetteer, Pg.: 867.
12. S. C. Roy, The Oraons of Chhotanagpur, op.cit, Pg.: 26
13. E. T. Dalton, Tribal History of Eastern India, Cosmo Pub. Delhi, 1973, Pg.: 245
14. S. N. Majumdar Shastri (ed.) Ancient India as described by Ptolemy, 2nd. Edition, Calcutta, 1927, Pg.: 53
15. R. R. Diwakar, Bihar Through the Ages, Orient Longman, Calcutta, 1959, Pg.:52. Quoted in Shahabad Gazetteer, opp.cit. Pg.:407
16. Buchanan, op.cit. Pg.: 407
17. L.S.S.O' Malley, Bengal District Gazetteer : Santhal Parganas, Logas Press, New Delhi, Reprint 1999, Pg.: 23-24
18. J. W. Mecrindle (ed.) Ancient India as described by Megasthenes and Arrian, Trubner and Co. London, 1877, Pg.: 134-35.

Chapter : Two

Tilka Manjhi

(Tilka Manjhi became a martyr, but the ideal of Swaraj established by him had always moved the tribal population. Encouraged by this ideal, the Santhal Hul 1855-56 faced dissension)

Tilka Manjhi has the pride of place as being the first martyr of Jharkhand. He had shot the then Collector of Bhagalpur August Cleveland with his arrow resulting in his death on 13th January 1785. The twenty year old Cleveland had been very popular among the British and other officers. This was a very big achievement of the revolutionaries against the Company rule. Cleveland had been after Tilka Manjhi and his organization in a very planned manner.

Tilka Manjhi was born on 11th February 1750. Right from childhood he had become a skilled archer and was a boy of keen intelligence. He used to finely analyse the difficulties coming in his way. He did not take long to understand the moves of the British and his conclusions used to be invariably right. Despite being young, Tilka's anti-British freedom policy influenced the youth of the neighboring village. The youth having the same opinion set up an organization. The aim of the organization was to drive away the British and establish their own rule. Gradually the number of such youths started increasing. Tilka Manjhi was elected the leader of the organization and all members took the vow to follow Tilka's orders.

At this juncture, it is necessary to consider an important point. Tilka Manjhi had died in the year 1785, and after his death the Santhals had come from various directions and settled in Dumka and other areas. The historians believe that the Santhals came and settled in Dumka and other areas in between 1790 and 1810.[1] Meaning[2] thereby that the Santhal of Damin-e-Koh had nothing to do with Tilka Manjhi. The Santhal tribe settled in Rajmahal had been the recipients of special beneficence of Cleveland.

The Govt. had freed this tribe from paying land rent. Among the Paharia tribe the village head or gram pradhan is called Manjhi

When Cleveland formed a semi-Govt. army of local people, then all the 1300 appointees were of Paharia tribe. This army was named as Hill-rangers A wicked dacoit (bandit) called Jaurrah was appointed as its head despite the fact that there had been comments about it. Cleveland, however, had his own arguments. Later on we will see that Tilka Manjhi was arrested by Jaurrah.

The distress of the zamindars

Tilka Manjhi had become a terror for the zamindars. The zamindars used to collect rent at a higher rate from the tenants. There used to be a special clerk for collecting rent and two to four musclemen to help him. At times situations used to arise when a tenant bound by rope was presented before the zamindar. Tilka Manjhi or some member of his organization would arrive at that place and then it would be sheer misery for the munshi (clerk) and his musclemen. Right at the time when the tenant was tied and being taken away by the munshi and his men, then, perchance if they met the members of that organisation then the tenant would be forcibly freed and warning would be given that if torture was increased then they would capture the zamindar.

Such incidents made Tilka Manjhi and his organization very popular. Amongst the population, Tilka Manjhi had become a hero. There was a beneficial fallout that if necessity arose, the villagers would come forward to protect him. The zamindars used to be afraid of Tilka Manjhi and his followers. No zamindar would come forward hence they felt nervous to send written complaint, but imvardly they all wanted his destruction. Despite this, in some way or the other information used to reach Collector Cleveland.[3]

Efforts to arrest

Bhagalpur's Collector Cleveland had prior to that worked among the Paharia tribes of Rajmahal and had become popular among them as Jhilmili sahib. Cleveland had deputed officers named Morell, Haber, Gabriel Heeler Asticott and Mitford to several specific villages of the Paharia tribe. He had attached 50 soldiers each, belonging to the semi-Govt. Paharia army, with these officers in the belief that they would be aware of the local conditions. They were armed the same way the enemy was armed. Cleveland fully hoped that Tilka would definitely be caught.

Across the jungle Mitford's armed troop was marching ahead amidst tall grasses. They were attacked with arrows and sling shots. Being injured, the soldiers ran helter and skelter. Most of the Paharia soldiers who nursed a fear of Tilka, were the first soldiers to make good their escape from the battlefield. They could see death on both sides. The arrows of Tilka rained as death in the battlefield, and if they returned to the cantonment they would be punished for being deserters. Mitford was shouting "Fire, fire," to the soldiers holding firearms and moving ahead when he was struck by an arrow and due to the injury he fell on the ground. The whole troop had scattered. How many had died, how many ran away and how many were shouting for help after being injured, there are no figures. This second effort of Cleveland also proved a failure. It was not easy to capture Tilka Manjhi.

Cleveland was of the view that the semi-Govt. Paharia troops did not have the swiftness which soldiers were supposed to have. One could not fully depend upon them. This time armed police were sent to capture Tilka Manjhi. Tilka Manjhi knew that this pursuit would be formidable. Tilka Manjhi's intelligence department was very skilful. His men used to keep an eye on the activities of the Collector. The men who worked as guides in the area, often, as per plan of Tilka Manjhi, used to take them on those paths or places where Tilka's men waited to ambush them.

After crossing the jungle when the police reached the plainsfull of tall grass, there were thickets and bushes on the edges. Suddenly, arrows were being shot. Police resorted to firing on the thickets and bushes. The arrows were being shot very expertly. Some got injured and some fell to the ground. Gradually the bullets of the police got exhausted. It seems that the men of Tilka Manjhi were waiting for this moment. Step by step the shooting of arrows increased and the police being injured were falling down. A time came when the field became completely clear. Those who were fleeing had already fled. Some were dead, and some were screaming in pain. In this way, the third attempt to catch Tilka Manjhi became fruitless.

The assassination of Cleveland

Tilka Manjhi despised the British but his despise for Cleveland turned into enmity. Cleveland wanted to catch Tilka Manjhi alive or else wanted to kill him in an encounter. With the passage of time and failure of Govt. attempts, Tilka was being deified among the tribal population. In addition, the zamindars lived in fear of him. The zamindars increased the pressure on Govt. to finish off Tilka.

On the other hand, Tilka wanted to kill Cleveland and spread fear among the British. He made preparations as per daily routine of Cleveland. He climbed up a palm tree with his bow and arrows. This palm tree stood on one side of the road, and Tilka hiding himself atop, waited for Cleveland. After some time Cleveland could be seen coming on horseback, and Tilka shot him in the chest with his arrow. Cleveland became injured and fell to the ground and very soon he died.[4] Tilka came down from the tree and returned home. This incident took place on 13th January 1784.

Tilka and his followers were celebrating this victory. Since it was night, they were free from anxiety regarding their enemies. But there were some tribals the same as them who were wanting to catch Tilka and were in hot pursuit of him. Ayercoot and Jaurrah, the sardar (captain) of the semi-Govt. Pahariya army raided the followers of Tilka when they were happily celebrating. Some followers got caught but Tilka escaped and took shelter in the hills of Sultanganj. Here also Tilka organized his army and trained them in guerilla warfare. He again became a challenge for Warren Hastings. But due to lack of adequate resources his organization could not be very energetic.

The hanging of Tilka

Sardar Jaurrah who himself was a notorious dacoit and whom Cleveland had appointed as captain of the semi-Govt. army, was in hot pursuit of Tilka Manjhi. At an opportune moment he caught Tilka Manjhi by deceit and handed him over to the authorities in Bhagalpur. In order to lower him in the eyes of the public and to terrify them, he was tied by rope to 4 horses and dragged on the road in full view of the crowd and thereafter hanged in public from the branch of a banyan tree.

Tilka Manjhi became a martyr, but his ideal of "swaraj" or self-rule always moved the tribal population which manifested itself in 1855-56 in the form of Santhal Hul. He was the first martyr of Jharkhand who was executed by hanging.

List of Reference books

1. L. S. S. O' Malley, Santhal Parganas District Gazetteer, second Indian Reprint, 199999, New Delhi, Pg.: 41.
2. O' Malley quotes Buchanan—— date of their settlement there may be placed between 1790 and 1810, Pg.: 9.
3. Ibid..... Commandant being one Jaurrah, once a noted bandit.... Pg.: 40.
4. Singh K. S., Tribal Society of India (An Anthropological History perspective) page 121.

Chapter : Three

Budhu Bhagat

(Budhu Bhagat, the hero of the first war of independence of the tribals of Jharkhand, had become a synonym for terror among the British. The British believed that if only Budhu Bhagat could be caught alive or dead, the revolt of 1831-32 would automatically die down).

Budhu Bhagat

In the history of Jharkhand, Budhu Bhagat was the first hero of the tribal war of independence in 1831-32. The freedom struggle began in village Ruchang of Sonepur when on 11 December 1831 one group of Mundas of that village raided contractor Mohammad Ali's Kuyam village and drove off with about 200 animals. On 20 December, about 700 Mundas in a violent group looted, plundered and set on fire 4 villages of Sonepur due to which 2 Sikhs were injured. These villages were of a Sikh contractor Hari Singh. The Mundas who were being oppressed by the contractors and zamindars, became determined to face them. The whole Munda country became ignited with the fire of revolt.

Prior to this, the Mundas of the valley had raised the flag of revolt against local oppression, but the revolt had been stamped out. The pain of the valley had remained suffocated within the valley. But this time, this did not happen. The fire of revolt crossed the valley and reached the plateau and Budhu Bhagat, by turning the revolt into a movement, had given it a fierceness.

Budhu Bhagat was born on 17 February 1792 in an ordinary Oraon family of Silagai village situated on the bank of River Koel in Chanho block, district Ranchi. From childhood he was a loner and thinker. Different from other boys of the village, he would, after taking his bath daily, sit on a stone on the bank of the River Koel. He was a fine archer. At times it seemed that while seated he was strolling about in a different world.

According to his co-villagers, divine powers had manifested themselves in him. One day after taking his bath, instead of returning home, Budhu Bhagat picked up his bow and arrows and went towards Barka Tongri. Coming near, he aimed at Tongri and shot an arrow. The arrow plunged into the Tongri and water spouted from that point. This incident was enough to create a reputation for Buddhu Bhagat. Word spread in the neighbouring villages that Budhu Bhagat had divine power. He was second to none not only as an archer but also in swordsmanship. As time passed, the number of Bhagat's supporters increased. Till the time of Kol revolt, this number had reached thousands.

The middle part and Budhu Bhagat

This revolt had developed in three phases. The first phase was of the area of the Mundas of the valley when the Mundas being oppressed by the contractors and zamindars had risen up in arms to take revenge. When this revolt crossed the valley of the Mundas and reached the area of the Oraons then its intensity lessened but it started spreading steadily. In addition to the Oraons, some big and important people had started helping the revolt, overtly or covertly. Officers likes Blunt, Russell and Dent who had at some time been connected with the area, fully believed that Nagpur's Maharaja Jagarnath Shahi was at the root of the revolt. They quoted the statement of Singrai Manki.[1]

Actually the Maharaja and the British Govt. were on very tense terms and when the revolt started, every-body who was against the British tried to take advantage. In this way, in Leslieganj, the Govt. official Gauri Charan and Alam Chand at their own level fully helped the rebels. Which means that in the middle part/phase, the revolt had turned into an effort to uproot the British govt. The Vice Chairman of Governor General Council Charles Metcalfe had accepted this truth.[2]

In this way, the form and aim of the revolt had undergone a change in the middle phase. The third phase of the revolt was in Daltonganj and nearby areas. Since in the middle phase the revolt was clearly seen to be an effort to end British rule, therefore, during the third phase some wharfingers and influential persons alongwith their supporters gave strength to the revolt.

It was the middle part of the revolt wherein the tribal revolt took on the appearance of the war of independence. To control this revolt, the army's help had to be taken. Budhu Bhagat was aware of army procedure; hence he trained his men accordingly.

Organizational Capability

Budhu Bhagat had wonderful organizational capability. He had kept every village in touch with each other. In whichever village he would be, he would get information about the activities of the enemy. Every village had an informant messenger whose run ended with the informant messenger of the next village. In those days, mountainous passes were important and the enemy's army often used the mountainous routes. Their way used to be obstructed by throwing stones and boulders or raining of arrows from above. Bhagat had advised the villages near those routes to be ready from before. Bhagat used to say that to the enemies our roads were unknown. They had to go somewhere but landed up some where else. This mistake at times used to prove fatal. But if we are not prepared, the enemy reaches us. We cannot fight face to face with the enemy. God has given us hills, mountain roads, jungles. We will shoot arrows at them but they will not be able to see us. We will definitely win if we adopt this style of fighting.

The spell of Budhu Bhagat had also overshadowed the British. The Joint Commissioner in his letter to the chief of the 50th Native Infantry had said that Budhu Bhagat is such a leader that one call from him will gather thousands of Kols.[3]

This revolt which began in December 1831 in Sonepur block of Chhotanagpur, moved through the area of the Oraons to Daltonganj and nearby areas from where after arousing them, it knocked on the border of Benaras (English daily, India Gazette, Calcutta, 10 February 1832). The revolt spread so far and wide had not become uncontrolled, especially till the limits of Chhotanagpur. The British and army officers believed that this revolt was being shouldered by one captain. Only through his arrest or death the whole revolt would scatter.[4]

In this way, Budhu Bhagat was at the centre of the entire movement. In fact the middle portion of the movement joins the first and last phases and works like the spinal column. But it is not the specialty of its being the middle part but the specialty of that master who gave a new direction to the revolt, a new meaning. Due to this new meaning some important people had helped it. This was a tribal effort to free the country from the British. The British administration from Calcutta to Chhotanagpur was troubled. Correspondence, meetings, discussions and many plans were made but Budhu Bhagat could not be caught. Information was received that Budhu Bhagat is present in a particular village but by the time someone reached there, there would be information that Budhu Bhagat had gone amidst the hills. The harassed officers and army men used to beat thee villagers as to why they let Bhagat get away. The villagers endured all torture of the British for the sake of Budhu Bhagat.

Divine Power

The water source emanating from Tongri was an incident which had become the basis of Budhu Bhagat's reputation that he was an extraordinary person and he was blessed with divine power. Later on events and Bhagat's nimbleness strengthened the superstition which was already there in the minds of the villagers. Budhu Bhagat's main field of operations was Choreya, Nagri, Tiko, Silagai, Pithoria and other nearby areas, yet he was well-known in other parts of Chhotanagpur as well.

Budhu Bhagat's area of operations was full of forests, hills, valleys, etc. i.e. natural hills and dales. Budhu was an expert horseman. He was aware of the long, short, dangerous short cut routes of his area. This was the reason why at one moment he would be seen in one village, and the next moment he would be in another village. Due to this extraordinary skill, the villagers thought him to be blessed with divine powers. His horse was familiar with all the routes and only a gesture from Budhu Bhagat was sufficient for it. As soon as Budhu Bhagat sat on the horse, it would fly off. This was the reason why he could be seen in two villages at the same time.

At that time, every household in the revolt affected villages was a "soldier." All able bodied persons were soldiers and they used to work according to instructions of the village chief. Budhu Bhagat used to change his places. The villagers firmly believed that Bhagat had divine powers and would be beyond the reach of the whites.

The anxiety of the British was increasing. Whenever the rebel group moved, there used to be 4-5 thousand persons in it. Despite having guns and cannon, the British troops would be perturbed in facing them because until there were enough soldiers and cavalry, facing the rebels would prove to be harmful. Captain impey had been given the task to capture Budhu Bhagat alive or dead. Captain lmpey chose Bhagat's area for military action. He asked for sufficient soldiers and cavalry men. The Captain reached Tiku with 6 companies of the 50th. Native Infantry which had come from Benaras, as also cavalry troops. According to Captain Impey, he captured 4000 rebels near Tiku and got them to surrender their weapons. But this claim of Impey appeared to be unnatural. With the arrival of Impey at Tiku, news about the coming of soldiers had spread in Tiku and nearby villages.

Rebels never directly face soldiers, they always favour guerrilla warfare. Considering the situation, if necessity arose, they would speedily vanish in the hills and forests. Hence, the incident of arrest of 4000 rebels was indeed surprising. Captain Impey does not speak about any fight with the rebels. At that time there was no village which did not have rebels. Hence it appears that searching for Budhu Bhagat, every house of Tiku and nearby villages was raided and tribal weapons kept at home were taken out, and declaring the house-holders to be rebels they were arrested. In this manner, the number of captive rebels had reached 4000, and they were being taken by Captain Impey to Choreya via the hilly route.

Howsoever it may be, but it is a fact that the captive tribals were from nearby villages and when they were going through the hilly road amidst the soldiers, their wives and children were beating their breasts and screaming. This was an injustice which Budhu Bhagat's followers had to endure. But the screams of the tribals did not go in vain. This incident is of 10 February 1832 A.D. In the month of February, suddenly thick clouds came over the valley and very soon the whole valley was lashed by a strong storm and heavy rain. In the hilly route the soldiers and horsemen were unable to control themselves let alone think about the captives. The captives had never seen such a terrible storm before. Taking advantage of the situation, the so-called rebel captives disappeared through the mountain routes. They were freed from Impey's unjust capture. What could be a better proof of divine powers ? This Budhu Bhagat ordered the rain and storm that "Go, free my tribal brothers from captivity" and the captives became free. Whatever, wherever, how so ever he wants, it happens accordingly. Impey and other British people were astonished at this incident and were compelled to think that Budhu Bhagat had something special in him.

Two edged sword

Budhu Bhagat was identified by his two edged sword and his horse. Although Budhu Bhagat was a skilful archer, yet whenever he was on horse-back, he would be accompanied by his double edged sword. Whenever Budhu Bhagat would wave his sword in the air, there would be dazzling light as of thunder. The onlookers would be bedazzled. The double edged sword of Bhagat was straight and slightly shorter than common swords. It was used at times of war but such an opportunity had not occurred in the recent past. Bhagat had a strong influence in all nearby villages. While sheathing the sword Bhagat would recite some incantation. No body knew anything about his incantation. Yet, Bhagat treated his sword with full honour and respect and never used it for small tasks. It is said that Chala Pachcho Devi had appeared and presented this sword to Bhagat. Bhagat's horse had been fully trained by Bhagat himself. It knew how to cross rivers and streams, how to climb up. People say that Bhagat's horse used to run at great speed. This was the reason why at one moment Bhagat would be seen in one village and the next moment he would be seen in another village. Bhagat could not move even one step without his horse. He used to take complete care regarding its food, water and rest.

Reward on his head

The Wilkinson administration had failed in its efforts in all manner but Bhagat could not be caught alive or dead. The people living in Bhagat's area were ready to sacrifice their lives in order to protect Bhagat.

In addition, there were high and low hills and thick forests wherein Bhagat would live incognito for sometime. The attack on Tiku by Captain Impey and the search for Bhagat amongst the Oraons went in vain. Bhagat could not be captured. Ultimately it was decided to give allurement of money. Possibly, enticed by money someone may inform the Govt. about Bhagat. Hence, the company government announced a prize money of one thousand rupees to anyone who would help in catching Budhu Bhagat dead or alive. In those days, one thousand rupees had great value.

Time passed but there was no information regarding Budhu Bhagat. Bhagat's life was more precious than money. Actually, Budhu Bhagat was such a simple person who had no enemies. Bhagat was Ajaatshatru, i.e. person having no enemy. In his own village Silagai, there was none envious or jealous of him. He was not only leader and patron of the race but also loved by everyone. Hence, all efforts of the British Govt. to catch Budhu Bhagat, used to fail.

Human wall

Captain Impey who had been camping along with his troops at Tiku, got information that Bhagat has come to his village. Captain Impey surrounded Silagai village with 4 companies of Infantry and cavalry. The infantry with drawn guns was moving towards the village while the horsemen came behind them. The village was in an uproar. The villagers knew that the encirclement had been done to catch Bhagat. Bhagat said, "I will surrender so that the destruction of the village can be stopped." But the villagers were admant that at any cost Bhagat had to be saved. The village had 300-350 persons who could face the army. It was decided that keeping Bhagat in the centre all the villagers would form four to five circles. In this way, protecting Bhagat by a human wall, he would be led away from the troops. This was certain that those who would face the troops, would have to face bullets.[5] They were planning to reach Bhagat to a safe place by facing bullets as solid rock and slaying the enemies.

But how long could swords and axes endure guns and pistols.[6] Very soon the whole village came under the grip of the soldiers. The huts had been burnt down. Children, the elderly and women had all come out. Bullets were being fired. The bullets did not know whom to hit. Budhu Bhagat, both of his sons Haldhar and Girdhar, brother and nephew and hundreds of his supporters were killed.[7] Silagai village was completely destroyed so that "any" Budhu Bhagat night not escape.

Now everything was quiet. The field was littered with corpses. In between some burning huts absolute silence had spread which from time to time would be disturbed by the weeping of unclad innocent children trying to find out their mothers from among the dead bodies. Or else, the screams of the mothers would tear the silence when, with babies tried to their backs, they tried to search their husbands among the corpses.[8]

Captain Impey had achieved a very big success. Due to this happiness of the success, one thousand rupees were distributed among the soldiers.[9] In addition, Impey wanted to send the information of the downfall of Budhu Bhagat alongwith proof to the main campsituated at Pithoria. So Budhu Bhagat, his brother and nephew were decapitated and their heads were sent in a plate to Pithoria camp. At that time the representative of Bengal Harkara was present in the camp. When the cloth from the covered heads was removed, the horrible and inhuman scene made his hair stand on end. He had not thought that the British race which is said to be civilized could be so barbarous. This was the height of barbarity.[10]

Information regarding the killing of Budhu Bhagat spread like forest fire everywhere. It seemed that the movement had become lifeless. Not only big influential leaders but village after village under the leadership of their pahan or mahto had started surrendering before the Commissioner.[11] They pledged loyalty to the British Govt. Such surrenders had a baneful effect in other areas. Some surrendered and some settled down peacefully. Till the end of April, the movement became lifeless.

The tribal revolt of 1831-32 had under the leadership of Budhu Bhagat taken a wider and important turn. Overtly or covertly, people had joined this movement. Some well-known British officials used to say with emphasis that the Maharaja of Nagpur was at the root of this revolt and with the help of the tribes wanted freedom from the British Govt. With the spread of the revolt people started joining it. There were also some people who had been working for the Company govt. but changed sides and went against the govt. for which they joined the revolt. Such people to become rebels and to come forward to shoulder the responsibility of leadership (Chamar Shahi and others) clarified the direction/mood of the movement. Historian P.C. Roy Choudhary has accepted this movement as the first war of independence of the tribals. Senior British officers have also said that the aim of the revolt was to throw out the British and to establish their own rule.

In this way, the tribal revolt of 1831-32 was actually the first war of independence of the tribals and Budhu Bhagat was the first martyr of this war.

But the re-volution of 1857 is that of zamindar of Pithoria Jagatpal Singh. Jagatpal Singh was a great British loyalist and a trusted person of Commissioner Dalton. He used to brief Dalton, positioned in Hazaribagh, about the incidents happening in Ranchi. Jagatpal Singh sent news that Ganpat Rai was being seen among the rebel soldiers for the past 5-6 days. Ganpat Rai was the Diwan of the Maharaja of Nagpur, but due to increasing distrust between the two, Ganpat Rai detached himself from the Diwani and returned to Bhowro and started looking after his zamindari work. When all the soldiers of Hazaribagh and Doranda revolted, then Ganpat Rai sent them a congratulatory letter. Pandeya Ganpat Rai of lean and thin body and dark complexion, was 45 years of age in 1857.[12]

List of reference books

1. Russel to Braddon, 18th April, 1832, Enclosure Singri Manki, quotes J.C.Jha, The Tribal Revolt of Chhotanagpur 1831-32, Patna, 1987, Pg.: 158, F.N.
2. Charles Metcalfe....... They (Coles) did intend to expel the British Govt. from their own country and establish their own independence.... Minute 14th April, 1832, Beng. Cr. Jude Cons no. 17th 18th June, 1832, WBSA.
3. J. C. Jha quotes Jt. Commissioner..... "so that large numbers could be assembled at a moment's notice, and they had in Budhu Bhagat of Silligaon, a leader with very great influence over them." Op.cit. Pg.: 108.
4. Ibid., "It was confidently expected that his (Budhu Bhagat) death or seizure would soon lead to the pacification of the area."
5. H. H. Spry, modern India, London, 1837, Vol. I, Pg.: 121-122
6. Major Sutherland, "The Buggat's family and followers stood up like men round their aged chief ...... " Bengal Hurkaru, 29th February, 1832.
7. Ibid.
8. J. C. Jha, "The old leader thus perished with his brother, sons and hundred followers" op.cit. Pg.: 109-110.
9. John Bull quoted in the Bengal Hurkaru, 2nd March, 1832,
10. H. H. Spry, op.cit. Pg.: 122.

11. Bengal Hurkaru, "I have to this instant seen the heads which have been brought in to the Commissioner's, how horrid it is to see such sights." 21 February, 1832.
12. Bengal Hurkaru, "The good effects arising from Buddoo Buggut's death are already visible, as the chiefs of many khole villages have come in and tendered their submission to the Commissioners." 29th February, 1832.

Chapter : Four

Poto Sardar

(In whichever country or race there are traitors, the freedom of that country or race is always in danger. Poto Sardar had given a difficult challenge to Thomas Wilkinson and he kept on wandering with his army from hilly road to hilly road. Ultimately some greedy traitors got Poto Sardar and his supporters captured through secret information. On New Year's day of 1838 they were executed by hanging.)

Poto Sardar

After entering Nagpur, the Mundas traditionally settled in the north-western part of the plateau. When the Oraons entered Nagpur, the Mundas gave up their place of settlement to the Oraons and went and settled in the plains of the south-eastern valley. Some of these Mundas spread towards the south and went and settled in the hills and forests near Singhbhum. They came to be known by their ancient name of "Ho". Due to their fighting nature, they became famous as "fighter Ho." Based upon their name, their country was called Kolhan. Kolhan is divided in "Peeds". 12-15 villages make one "peed." The speciality of Kolhan is that it is madeup of high and low hills and mountainous paths. The Hos used to protect themselves with the help of these hills and forests, and the British forces going through those mountainous passes had to endure showers of poisonous arrows. The main reason of the invincibility of the Hos was the natural geographical structure of Kolhan. Still then, the local rajas and the British officers had easily acknowledged the bravery and courage of the Hos. Martyr Poto Sardar was born in Kolhan and prospered there.

Poto had seen the Ho revolt of 1819-20. He had been influenced by the echo of the Kol (tribal) revolt. Thomas Wilkinson, the agent of the Governor General, had called a "hill assembly" at Seraikela on 8 June 1833 to assess the participation of Larka Ho of Singhbhum in the revolt 1831-32 and to know the root cause of the revolt. Most of the Mankis and Mundas of Kolhan attended the assembly.[1] The aim of Wilkinson was to find out the reasons of the revolt. The Mankis of Kolhan advised that whatever happened should be forgiven and forgotten. This assured Wilkinson. Although Wilkinson knew that the Hos of Kolhan had played a very effective role in the spread and heat of the revolt of 1831-32 and that the Ho tribe was not a tribe to remain quiet, yet he vowed to thrust his authority over Kolhan and to educate them. He had been informed about Kolhan being disturbed and in mid 1836- he had wanted to surround Kolhan. This encircling by Wilkinson started in November 1836 and by February 1837 it was over.[2] Nearly all Mankis accepted British rule. Lieutenant Tecail, who was liberal and nature-loving,[3] took over the responsibility of administration of Kolhan.

Every thing was quiet on the surface but the Ho tribe which was traditionally used to a free life started feeling unbearable suffocation. Poto of Rajabasa peed found many of his comrades suffering from this problem. Bora and Deeb of Baldiya, Potel, Gopali, Pandua, Nara, Barai of Palsa village alongwith 20-25 tribal comrades were prepared with some weapon or the other. Very soon, sufferers from other villages pledged their support to Poto. In a few days, Kolhan got a strong squad of Martyrs. The Hos who under stood the value of independence, were ready for the new fight for independence. Along with Lalgarh, Awla, Barh, Peed, the people of about 22 villages were ready to revolt against the rule of the British. Steadily, with more people joining this revolt, it took on the form of a public movement. Along with Kolhan, this movement spread from Seraikela to Keonjhar district in Orissa.

To make this movement a success, Bhaguni Naik of Barbil, Orissa, joined it. Bhaguni Naik was known to be having supernatural powers with unlimited power in his incantations. His name was famous not only in Keonjhar but also in Seraikela and Kolhan. Under the leadership of Poto, alongwith Naik, Tepoy of Balondia, Koye and Vardan of Sarbil, and Pandua, Jotong and Jonkar of Pata Dumariya were the mighty warriors who jumped into the movement. Due to the association of these famous fighters, the movement received fresh strength.[4]

Secret meetings

It was clear that at the present moment when the British had gained power over Kolhan, they would not have a soft approach towards it. The spies and other employees of the British were used to gather information regarding unrest in the Kolhan. Under the circumstances it was necessary to control the movement and to give it a proper direction, hence secret meetings had to be held. Till that time, meetings used to take place in Pokam village but the British authorities had been informed about Pokam village. Thus a new secret centre was made in Walindia village near Mariya. In a secret meeting held here under the chairmanship of Poto, decisions was taken[5]:

1. To take revenge on the British for those who were killed or whose houses were set on fire by them through rain of bullets or arson indulged in the period from November 1836 to February 1837 in the Kolhan.
2. Take possession of the mountainous passes of Serengsia and Bagliya which were important from a tactical point of view.
3. Drive out all the British and others from the land of Kolhan.
4. And, include the other people of that area in the struggle and by sending arrows to other villages invite them to drive out the foreign enemies.

Keeping the aforesaid aims in mind, Poto Sardar re-organised the freedom loving Kolhan residents. Captain Thomas Wilkinson had seen the strong role of the "fighter" Ho in the tribal revolt of 1832 and he was of the firm belief that peace would be difficult to maintain in the tribal region unless and until the Kolhan came under the total grip of the Govt. Wilkinson's surmise was proved correct.

The fire of Kolhan subjugation in February 1837 had still not quietened down when thousands of Ho armed with traditional weapons stood up for the freedom of Kolhan under the leadership of Poto Sardar. Wilkinson had commented about the previous revolt saying that apart from some people flaunting their leadership for some time, nothing else would result from such revolts.[6] But he was wrong in his assessment. Nobody sacrifices his life just for flaunting his leadership. No pretender sacrifices his life. This was a band of martyrs. It is possible that Wilkinson may have commented just to boost the morale of his colleagues because to put down this revolt he had to take help from various sources.

The area of Singhbhum lay within the South West Frontier Agency. Most of the administrative problems of Singhbhum were connected to Kolhan. After receiving news of revolt of Poto Sardar, these were taken with ease, and order to arrest him was issued. But Poto Sardar and his supporters continued with their programme. The local officials were of the view that Poto Sardar had become the symbol of the independence of Kolhan. He had widespread support of the population. Due to his influence, the whole of Kolhan was again facing upheaval. It was necessary to send troops.

On 12 November 1837 after consulting Chaibasa and local authorities, Thomas Wilkinson decided to send troops under the command of Captain Armstrong to put down the rebels.

Captain Armstrong started for Barh Peed on 17 November 1837 along with 2 cannons, 400 armed soldiers and 60 cavalry. The Raja of Seraikela provided 200 soldiers for this expedition, while the zamindar of Bankura was ordered to remain in preparedness.

Armstrong along with his troops went ahead without any hindrance. On 19 November 1837 when the British troops were in the midst of Serengsiya mountain pass, suddenly they were attacked with poisonous arrows. This pass is surrounded on both sides with hills and the soldiers of Armstrong had no idea regarding the forest path. It was difficult for them to save themselves. Many soldiers and horses either died or were injured. This was the first defeat of the British troops.

Wilkinson felt it necessary to increase the strength of his troops. He immediately asked Manki Lakshman Singh of Terai and Manki Bala Singh of Sagundih to send 100-100 soldiers. He also asked the zamindar of Keydar and the Thakur of Kharsawan to send troops at once. Reinforced with new troops, the first attack on Poto Sardar took place at Raja Lakha peed. The soldiers took the father of Poto Sardar in custody and set the village on fire probably thinking that another shelter of Poto Sardar or his men should be destroyed.

Due to this wrong information that the rebels were hiding in Taraghatu, 100 soldiers and some cavalry men surrounded Taraghatu village on all four sides, but the soldiers got nothing except 60 women who were arrested and the village was set on fire from all sides. The whole village was burnt to ashes.

The growing barbarity of the British troops had crossed all limits of endurance. It was not known how the British benefited from killing innocent people, indulging in arson, and destruction of village and food grains. Ultimately the freedom fighters decided to face frontal attack of the British troops, so they resolved to challenge the enemy between the villages of Jaipur and Ruia. But before they could reach Ruia village, the British soldiers surrounded them. It was a matter to ponder as to which traitor had informed the British about the place of presence of the rebels. Based on the secret information, Lieutenant Tickell started surrounding, with a part of the army, from the direction of Jaipur village, while Captain Armstrong and Lieutenant Simpson started surrounding the rebels from the side of Ruia village accompanied by 300 soldiers from Ramgarh battalion. Although some freedom fighters were caught, some others, especially the leaders, escaped.

Thomas Wilkinson thought it to be half a success. According to him, till Poto Sardar and the other leaders were not caught, Singhbhum would always remain restive. Wilkinson demanded from Fort William Govt. the power to prosecute the rebels and, as per requirement and seriousness of charges, to execute them. The company Govt. acceded to the demand. Thereafter Wilkinson became more empowered and was authorized by the Govt. to give death sentence.

Captain Thomas Wilkinson was thought to be a very successful officer. On one hand he had harshness and on the other, humbleness. Wilkinson policy was a coordination of both. He had talks with some traitorous rebels and made them true loyalists of the Company Govt. Some rebels out of greed passed on information of secret places of Poto and the other rebels to the British officials and helped them to arrest the rebels. This is an old saying that the foundation of British rule in India had been the result of internal treachery and treason. This was a basic equalizing factor.

The same thing happened with the freedom fighters of Kolhan. Intensive raids at places identified by betrayers resulted in the capture of principal revolutionaries like Bodo, Naro, Badai and Pandya in Singhbhum in 1837. On 8 December 1837 Poto and his colleague Deeway were caught by the British. These freedom fighters went through summary trial in the court of Wilkinson at Jagannathpur from 18 December 1837 to 25 December. On 31 December 1837 judgment of the case was delivered. Poto, Bodo, Pandua, Naro and Badai were sentenced to death and the remaining rebels were sentenced to various prison terms. By that time Wilkinson had been vested with the power of death sentence.

On 1 January 1838, Poto, Nara and Badai were hanged in front of a huge crowd in Jagannathpur. This was an easy way to terrorise the public of Jagannathpur which was taken recourse to by Wilkinson and his colleagues. Wilkinson, during his service tenure, had started execution by hanging from the New Year. Accordingly, on 2 January 1939, the administration hanged Bodo and Pandua in front of a public gathering at Serengsiya.

The sacrifice of Poto and his colleagues did not go in vain. Within 2 decades in 1857 the Kolhan area of Singhbhum revolted again. The tradition of martyrdom established by Poto had remained alive in the land of Kolhan. Thomas Wilkinson had given a New Year's gift to the Company Govt. by hanging Poto Sardar on 1 January 1838. In India, probably Ho tribes can be singled out which from ancient times to modern times have not accepted the supremacy of any empire.

Amongst the British officers, Thomas Wilkinson was acknowledged to be the most efficient officer. He used to adopt the policy of sympathy and respect along with war. He was a supporter of "Munro" school of thinking. He was the agent of the widespread jurisdiction of south west frontier Agency and directly responsible to the Governor- General for his work. In the interest of good administration, Wilkinson had wanted, just like the Nizam court, the power to sentence a convict to 14 years' rigorous imprisonment.[7] The Company Govt. had vested this power in him.

After settling the Kol Revolt, Agent Wilkinson tried to control the fighter "Ho" of Singhbhum in such a manner that they would not be able to revolt again. Wilkinson had observed that after completing the prison sentence of 8-10 years, the revolutionaries on return to their village got more respect and influence. He thought that such political rebels should be punished as per their crime or hanged for the crime of sedition, but at that time Wilkinson did not have the power to hang a convict. During the time of annexation of Kolhan, in 1837 he requested the Company Govt. to empower him with the authority to punish by hanging. Kolhan was burning in 1837. Just like Poto Sardar, some other fighter "Hos" had wanted to free Kolhan from the British. Greedy spies informed the British about Poto Sardar and his colleagues. Vested with the power to punish by hanging, Wilkinson used this power for the first time to punish Poto Sardar and his colleagues on 1 January 1838. Wilkinson had given a ghastly New year's gift to the Company Govt.

Along with the punishment by hanging, probably Poto Sardar created history by being the first martyr of Chhotanagpur who underwent execution by hanging.

Agent Wilkinson had been empowered by the Company to punish by hanging so that the freedom fighters could be curbed and wiped out forever. He had used this power for the first time on Poto Sardar. At that time, Wilkinson was the highest authority in Chhotanagpur and he did not have the power to sentence by hanging. He had to request the Company for this power. The circumstances make it clear that Poto Sardar was the first victim of Wilkinson. It is also evident that prior to Poto Sardar no freedom fighter had been sentenced to death by hanging in Chhotanagpur. Tilka Manjhi was from an area outside Chhotangpur and the remarkable point about the

Martyrdom of Budhu Bhagat is that he was killed twice, by gun shot in the battle field due to which he fell the ground and, againt, he was beheaded. After Budhu Bhagat comes Poto Sardar among the martyres of Chhotanagpur who were executed by hanging. It is evident from the then circumstances that among the martyrs of Chhotanagpur pride of place goes to Poto Sardar who was the first freedom fighter to step up to the noose and kiss it before hanging.

List of Reference Books

1. P. Kumar, Mutinies and Rebellions in Chhotanagpur (1831-1857) Patna, 1991, Pg.: 89.
2. Ibid.
3. Singhbhum Gazetteer, Patna, 1958, Pg.: 8
4. J.A.S.B., 1840, Pg.: 696
5. Singhbhum Gazetteer, Annexation of the Kolhan, Pg.: 87-88
6. Ibid, "The men who it appeared desirable to make an example of, in consequence of their having been leaders in the previous disturbances, were given up or captured...." Pg.: 87-88.
7. J. C. Jha, op.cit. Pg.: 249

Chapter: Five

Siddhu and Kanhu

("We have been ordered by Marang Buru to establish our rule")

Siddhu and Kanhu

Santhal Pargana is the north-eastern part of the land of Jharkhand, the mother of the brave. Santhal Pargana is famous for its glorious history. A golden chapter of this history is the Santhal Revolt of 1855-56. This revolt was the struggle of Santhals and comrades to win freedom from the British and to establish "Abua Raj" (self rule), which the historians called "Santhal Hul" meaning Santhal revolt, but actually it was a freedom struggle by the tribal community of a limited area. The leader of this freedom struggle was the brave and learned Siddhu and his younger brother Kanhu of Bhagnadih. Armed with bows-arrows and hatchets, more still, the complete support of the population behind their area, they fought against the exploiters who were armed with cannons and guns and who were being backed by the exploitative Company Govt. A time had come when the whole Pargana had come under the victory flag of Siddhu and Kanhu. But ultimately they had to face subjugation. There is no dearth of "Mir Jafars" in this country. Secret information was passed on to the British Compaany on the basis of which both were captured. In order to terrorise the general public, Siddhu and Kanhu were punished by hanging on 26 July 1856 at Barhet and Bhognadih respectively. These brave sons not only became immortal Martyrs of Santhal Pargana but also in the history of Jharkhand.

As usual, the British officials and historians confusing the truth of the freedom struggle of the Santhal revolt, termed it as the anger of half civilized tribals against the exploitation and torture of the moneylenders, zamindars and the police.[1] The historians have not said that it was against the British govt.[2] This is a one sided opinion. The atrocities of the money-lender,

Zamindar and police may have been one reason but the main reason was the freedom loving nature of the Santhals. Based on these facts, it has to be accepted that the importance of martyrdom of Siddhu and Kanhu can be assessed by considering the following points :

1. Santhal Pargana and Santhal
   (a) Entry into Santhal Pargana and settling down
2. The development of leader
   (a) Tribal tragedy
   (b) The feeling of "we" i.e. inclusiveness
3. Religious fundamentalism (agitation)
   (a) Thakur's order
4. Proclamation and departure, martyrdom

(1) Santhal Parganas and Santhal :

In addition to its geographic and natural distinctiveness, present day Santhal Pargana has always been important in the annals of Indian history. In ancient times this area surrounded by hills has been appropriate shelter for defeated tribes. The ancient tribe of "Maler" or Pahariya looking out for a safe and secure place had come and settled down in this hilly area. The famous Greek historian Megasthenes has mentioned Maler as "Mali" in his book "Indica."[3] Megasthenes had come to the court of Chandragupta in 302 B.C. In the early years of primeval times, the hills of Rajmahal and the lower plain had been under the influence of Maler. During Mughal times, the subedar of Bengal, Man Singh had annexed Raj Mahal. It has been proved that the Maler tribe of Rajmahal and the Oraon tribe of Chhotanagpur are uterine tribes. Till their life in Rohtasgarh, both had the same ancestors. While escaping from Rohtasgarh, they became divided into two groups. One group moved along the bank of the river Ganga and reached Rajmahal and was called Maler while the other group crossed the river Koel and entered Chhotanagpur via Palamau and came to be called Oraon. The descriptive writing of Megasthenes confirms the settling down of Oraon tribe in Chhotanagpur in 4th century B.C. Seeing the natural and social circumstances, Man Singh had made Rajmahal the capital of Bengal. Shah Shuja also liked Rajmahal. Rajmal proved to be life giving to the East India Company. The Company used to keep one office at Rajmahal. We know that the overflowing river Ganga after hitting the hills of Rajmahal goes towards Bengal and becomes an easy waterway for Calcutta and North India for trade. Rajmahal used to control this riverine waterway. Hence, the continued existence of East India Company and its other activities depended on the pleasure of Rajmahal. This was the same Rajmahal where Shah Shuja by giving the benefit of free trade to the Company broadened its road to become strong in India. Hence, for the Company govt. the Santhal Pargana route became very important both militarily and trade wise.

Santhal entry and settling down

The latest tribe to enter Sathal Parganas was the Santhal. According to historian, for the first time this tribe moved to the northern direction from Birbhumi and came and settled in Dumka district in between 1790-1810. This place was thickly forested and full of challenges for the industrious and experienced Santhals. They cut down the forest, cleared the area from fierce and violent creatures, and made the land cultivable. The local Zamindar and English authorities were pleased with their industry and bravery. As per Mister Sutherland, the Santhal had been seen busy in clearing the thick forest on the hills of Godda in 1818. Till 1827 they had been found to have settled down in the extreme northern end of Godda. In 1836 the report of the Collector of Bhagalpur Sri Denver was placed before the authorities in 1836 in which at least Santhali, Damini-i-Koh villages numbering 423 had been found although some villages were also of the Bhuiyas.

Actually, the Company Govt. by using the courage and industry of the Santhals wanted this area to be cleared. As per British authorities, making the forest land cultivable, this would not only benefit the tribes but there would be increase in the collection of land rent which would augment the resources of the Govt. Inspired by this idea, the Company Govt. posted Sri Pontet as Special Officer in Santhal Parganas on 21 November, 1836. Sri Pontet would encourage the Santhals to turn the jungle land into cultivable land, and he as Special Officer, would protect the interests of the Santhals.[4] Encouraged by Sri Pontet, the Santhal people went on spreading in Santhal Parganas. In confronting them, the lazy and careless hill-tribes could not pose any special obstruction. They gradually entered the deeply forested hill pass of Barhait and driving out the wild ferocious animals, they became successful in completely changing Barhit, the heart of Rajmahal.[5] Capt. Sherwill, after viewing in 1851 the heart of Rajhamal i.e. Barhait and its hill pass, had noted- "This pass/road, which had been surrounded by hills, with the help of sthe tribals in cutting down the forest, has changed into hundreds of Santhali villages. Now the beauty of this hill pass is to be seen to be believed. The Santhals here have vast cattle weath and are surrounded by crop growing agricultural fields which prove that they are completely well-off."[6]

As per a survey in 1857, the Santhals possessed 451744 bighas of land from which an amount of 47555 rupees used to be collected as land rent. But in the meantime the population of Santhals increased and in between 1838-51 their population stood at 82795 from 3000.[7] In addition to this, on the outer limit of Damin-e-Koh about 10000 Santhals had settled down. Compared to this increasing population, the land availability was very little. As a result, for most Santhals the means of livelihood was not agriculture but labour. It was a difficult circumstance that arrangements be made to give employment to all.

(1) Tribal Tragedy and rise of leaders

Before the rise of leaders, the life of the Santhal tribe had been full of tragedy. Nearly every British historian, Christian missionary and Govt. official has presented the tragedy of Santhali life in his own way. Their effort had been to present the Santhal movement as not against the Govt. but against the moneylender, zamindar, and junior employees which would divide entire Santhal Pargana as Santhali and non-Santhali. By proving that the reason for the anger of the Santhal was the zamindar, money lender, etc. these historians or officials tried to present a clean picture of the Company Govt. L. S. S. O'Malley while throwing light on the Santhal revolt, has given the following reasons :

Lies, Neglect of the Officers (Sahebs), Exploitation by Moneylenders, Atrocities of the Govt. lower employees and the police.[8]

In addition to L. S. S. O'Malley, J. B. Bredley Bert, W. W. Hunter, A. C. Widwel and others have thrown light on the revolutionary tribals and their tragedy, and the rise of the leaders. All of them feel that Santhals had been so much exploited and tortured that they wanted to free themselves from the then circumstances. The rise of Siddhu-Kanhu was for gathering public support against such exploitations and atrocities. Hence, the circumstances which were the reason for the rise of leaders were the following as per British historians and officials :

W. W. Hunter throwing light on the reasons for the rise of leaders (Siddhu-Kanhu) has expressed his own opinion. His book "Annals of rural Bengal."[9] was published in 1864. He has tried to prove in a basic way that the Santhals picked up arms in 1855-56 against the torture and exploitation by the Hindus. Hunter has openly and freely used the word "Hindu." In his opinion, those who are non-tribals are Hindus. In this context he has presented some examples :

If a Santhali required a loan, he would go to the Hindu (moneylender) from whom he would take a loan on 33 % compound interest. Since he would not have land or articles to mortgage, he used to pledge his services to the moneylender. In this way, in trying to payback the loan amount alongwith compound interest, his life would be over, and his children would inherit the slavery of the moneylender. According to Hunter, this bonded slavery would continue from generation to generation as a disease.[10]

Hunter has mentioned the exploitation and deceitfulness of the Hindu (Bania) and has described how the Hindu Bania used to cheat the Santhals in exchange of goods. The Bania used to take recourse to heavy weights when accepting some goods and to lighter weights when giving goods. In addition to this, if a Santhal took rice on credit from the Bania then a day would come when a Govt. employee would come to his house to take away his cattle for auction.[11]

According to Hunter, the facility of court was hardly available to the poor Santhals. More often, the court would be situated at a distance of 100 miles from the Santhal village due to which it was hardly possible for the Santhals to reach it. Again, the British officials had more interest in collecting land revenue hence they did not have time to solve the problems and difficulties of the Santhals. Thus it was that there was nobody to hear the complaints of the poor Santhals.[12]

Hunter, taking the side of the Company Govt. has written that the Company Govt. did not have information about the atrocities being committed on the Santhals. Hunter has used the word "Hindu" in a big way to denote the perpetrators of atrocities. This usage indicates that divisive policy of the British administration which had always been its part. However, Santhals got the support of Lohars who worked day and night to produce their arrows and swords for the revolt. Other Hindus had also helped them.

Compared to Hunter, A.C. Bidwell's study is more objective and researched. The aim of Bidwell was to collect information about the revolt from the various classes of people in society. Bidwell has tried to present a clear picture of the rise of the leaders.

A.C. Bidwell had been appointed as Special Commissioner by the Govt. to suppress the Santhal revolt.[13] Bidwell had tried to obtain the opinions of various classes of people of the area regarding the reasons for the rise of the leaders and rebels. Bidwell was certain about the exploitation of the Santhals and the atrocities committed by the money leaders upon them. He has cited as example in his letterthe report of Captain Sherwill that during the revolt 50 Bengali money lenders were killed. They were of Barhe, capital of Damin. Apart from this, the Bengali moneylenders of Borio had also been killed.[14] The atrocities committed by the moneylenders may have been one of the reasons for the Santhals to pick up arms against the administration. But the tribals awakening was the result of not one reason but other important reasons which inspired and encouraged the Santhals for freedom struggle. Some opinions are as below :

Charles Warnes

Sri Charles Warnes was involved for many years with indigo plantation and he had good knowledge of the behaviour and nature of the Santhals. Warnes was of the opinion that the rise of leaders Siddhu-Kanhu and others was due to religious fanaticism only. He had straightaway rejected the premise that zamindar, moneylender or atrocities by police had been the reason for their revolt. Sri Warnes opined that the Santhals were under the protection of the zamindar and they were so peace loving that they had never seen police or police station. According to him, some anti-social elements had blown up the religious fanaticism of the Santhals to fulfil their own interests.[15]

According to the Raja of Maheshpur, the increase in land rent, exploitation by the money lenders, atrocities by the railway managers (giving less payment and taking more work) and similar circumstances were responsible for the advantage which Siddhu-Kanhu availed of. The atrocities committed on the tribals played the main role in the awakening and development of the leaders.[16]

Tyler

Sri Tyler was an engineer in the Department of Railways, and he had close contact with the Santhal labourers. He has given various arguments regarding the reason for the rise of the leaders and the Santhal tribe to pick up arms. He has denied this statement that the labourers used to be paid less labour charges. According to him, Santhals were monetarily well off still the Govt. burdened them with increased Govt. rent. The Santhals were industrious and after imbibing alcohol would go above the mundane world. Tyler has said that some cunning Santhalis by using the name of "Thakur" had excited the religious fervour of the Santhals. These leaders were Siddhu and Kanhu.[17]

Babu Giridhari Kol

Babu Giridhari Kol was a Govt., pleader and zamindar. He has opined that the Santhals used to drink heavily and had become lazy. Their behaviour had become fanatical. Some ounning people had excited the feelings of the Santhalis and told them to murder, plunder and set up their own rule.[18]

From the aforementioned examples it is known that the revolt took place due to the money lender, zamindar and the exploitation of the labourers by the contractors, but these are routine examples. The main reason was to drive out the British govt. and setup home rule and for this Siddhu-Kanhu took the help of religion.

In this way, the exploitation and atrocities of the moneylenders, as also greater land rent, unavailability of justice, atrocities of the police etc. were several reasons for the disquiet among the tribes. These reasons helped in the rise of the leaders and were supportive issues because everybody wanted change.

We feeling

There was wonderful unity among the Santhal tribe. They used to feel as one with each other. This “we feeling” ran very deep. A single voice could attract all Santhalis. Due to such a nature, they could achieve success in a big way to collect gathering and get a community work done. The call of Siddhu-Kanhu for a public gathering resulted in people coming over to Bhagnadih in thousands as soon as information reached them. They pledged to do or die at the call of their leaders. 30 June 1855 which witnessed a gathering at night is a proof of this.

Religious fanaticism

The religious fanaticism of the Santhalis played a positive role in the rise of popular leaders. The gathering of the people in the name of religion and to obey the order of Thakur was necessary. Siddhu and Kanhu had told the public that they had been commanded by Thakur that they should destroy the tyrants and establish their own rule. On 30 June 1855, Siddhu and Khanu declared home rule and in the role of an administrator gave information about the appointment of officials to the public gathering.[19] The public gathering acknowledged the same by thunderous clapping of hands.

The Santhals were a tribe who were ready to die for the sake of their religion. The religious fanaticism of the tribe at times could be seen as religious frenzy. Some scholars affirming that the religious fanaticism of the Santhals influenced the rise and development of the leadership of Siddhu-Kanhu.

The Rise of the Leaders

In contemporary tribal society a belief regarding leaders was in vogue that whatever the leader is doing, actually that is an order of God which has to be followed by the people of the tribe as a religious duty. A similar incident had taken place with Siddhu-Kanhu. "Marangburu" had himself appeared before Siddhu-Kanhu and had given the order that they should drive away the distress of the Santhalis and set up Santhali Rule.

Siddhu and Kanhu were one night discussing at home the then painful condition of the tribe when suddenly a piece of paper fell on the hand of Siddhu. Before Siddhu could understand anything, God "Marangburu" of the sky came and revealed himself. Both brothers looked at him with stupefied eyes. The revealed personality was in tribal dress and absolutely white. Both his hands had ten fingers each. He had with him a white book. Alongwith the book, there were five sets of 20-20 pages. The book and paper were given to Siddhu. The figure went up to the sky and there after disappeared. After some time another piece of paper fell from the sky and came to rest on Siddhu's head. Very soon 2 human beings came from the sky and appeared before Siddhu-Kanhu. Each of their hands had six fingers. They both explained to Siddhu-Kanhu the reason for Marangburu to descend on earth, and after telling them about Thakur's order, they went away to the sky and soon they disappeared there.[20]

Till that time, God of Santhali religion had been invisible. The appearance of "Marangburu" and giving of order to Siddhu-Kanhu was a horripilating incident for the whole Santhal tribe. Some people started reaching Siddhu-Kanhu's home. Sticking the heavenly piece of paper to a sal twig, message was sent through it to all directions. Very soon, village to village and thereafter the whole Santhal area was filled with horripilation. The will to do something began to be aroused among the Santhals. They wanted to discuss the matter among themselves and to take decisive step. The future activities of the movement had to be joined. For this work, the full moon night of 30 June, 1855 was considered to be suitable.

Proclamation

Now the time had come when the eminent leaders had necessarily to clarify the full situation of the revolt before their brethren. On 30 June 1855 a huge public gathering was arranged in Bhognadih.

Addressing the public gathering, Siddhu called upon them to drive out money lenders, police, zamindar etc., including all such elements, from the Santhal area. These exploiters are the reason for the poverty of the Santhals.

We will have to progress in a systematic manner. Siddhu declared home rule in the assemblage and accordingly informed them about some appointments for the same.

The opinions expressed by the various Santhalis in this gathering make it clear that this movement of the Santhali was against the moneylenders, police officials and zamindars no doubt, but the main aim was to set up "Abua Raj." Comments of contemporary Govt. officials on this issue have come to light but they have taken the side of the Govt. declaring the revolt as against the money lender and police only. The pain caused by the Govt. was not mentioned.[21]

Approximately more than ten thousand Santhalis participated in the public gathering at Bhognadih. There are some people who have tried to under mine the importance of the movement by reporting lesser attendance in the gathering. Dr. Dutta according to the description of "Panch Kathiya" has quoted the figure at ten thousand.[22] Although Hunter has every time named Hindus as the exploiters and oppressors of the Santhalis, Hunter actually meant the bania and moneylender. The Lohar community of the Hindus worked day and night to make the movement a success. The rebels could get bows and arrows, spears etc. arms with the co-operation of the Lohars. In the view points expressed in the public meeting, the money lenders, zamindars, and even Govt. officials were criticized who were unable to get justice for the Santhals. But the main aim of the movement was "Swaraj" i.e. home rule.[23] Step by step the public assembly was ready for its Calcutta drive. All the Santhals armed with their weapons started from Bhognadih. At first they paid obeisance to the Goddess situated in the bazar of Panchkathiya. Thereafter they proceeded for Barhait. The public gathering at Barhait was unprecedented. Santhals walking all the way from forests, hills and faraway places participated in this meeting. The proclaimed aims of Bhognadih were re-iterated in this gathering and stress was laid on the setting up of Santhal Raj. Decisions regarding the future programme of the drive and other work were taken.

Leadership-Craft

The leadership of Siddhu-Kanhu ware very straight and clean. The first thing was the problem of keeping control over the vast multitudinous procession. That is why the procession was divided in several parts for which small leaders had been appointed. Siddhu was of very quiet bent of mind and also a very sober youth. He was worried about the difficulty in shepherding such a big population in the same way of thinking. Resultantly,

Kanhu and Siddhu used to meet most of the people, and tried to be in contact with the youth who were at the root of the movement. There was no place for anger. Siddhu knew that in order to give a bad name to the movement, the British Govt. would describe it as looting and plundering dacoits. That is why wherever Siddhu drew up a programme to visit any area, he would give prior information to the higher English authorities of that area. He had a wonderful speaking capacity. He used to mesmerise thousands of people through his words. All the rich and poor people of Santhal Pargana used to love and respect Siddhu-Kanhu. They were expert leaders.

The Murder of the Daroga

On 7th July, 1855 Maheshlal Dutt, daroga of Digghi, and his subordinate Sajawal, both on horseback, met the crowd in order to stop its drive. They wanted to make them understand that whatever be their demands would be fulfilled, but at that time rumour spread among the crowd that the Daroga had come to catch both brothers. The crowd became agitated and it caught the Daroga and his assistant, bound them with ropes and brought them before Siddhu. A court was set up to decide the future of the Daroga. Siddhu heard both sides. Death sentence was passed on the Daroga and his assistant.

The drive of the Santhalis moved on.

Attack on Pakur Raj

Gacho Manjhi had old enmity with Pakur Raj. The men of the Raj had insulted him. When information reached about the arrival of the Santhalis, there was panic everywhere in Pakur Raj. People shifted their wives and children to protected places. For this the house of the zamindar was thought to be suitable. Siddhu and Kanhu alongwith their Santhal brethren reached Pakur on 8th July 1855. The people of Pakur had been full of anxiety about their safety. Most of the people had taken refuge in the Maharaja's mansion. Siddhu surrounded the entire mansion. This went on till 12 July 1855. On 12th July, Siddhu-Kanhu along with some supporters entered the mansion but they were disappointed. The Raja along with his family and property had gone away to a different place. Thereafter Siddhu came out of the mansion. There were some sick persons, especially women, in the mansion, to whom they gave food and money. Their nature was to win appreciation and popularity among the public. Siddhu moved away from the mansion on 12 July. The next target was Maheshpur Raja.

Maheshpur

The Govt. had received information about the Santhali attack on Pakur Raj. The Santhals were spread in groups from south to north and from east to west. Every group was under the influence of the leadership of Siddhu-Kanhu. The Santhals walked from Pakur and reached Maheshpur. There they wholly ransacked and looted Rajmahal.[24] On 15th July when the Santhals started moving, singing victory song, they were confronted by the Seventh Regiment Native Infantry. At that time the number of Santhalis was 3000-4000. Similarly a part of the regiment reached the bank of the river Tarai which flows near Pakur. There 200 soldiers faced 5000 rebels. Of what avail were bows-arrows, hatchets-swords against bullets-guns ! very soon, the banks of the Tarai river were covered with the dead bodies of the rebels. Approximately 200 Santhals were killed, and a huge number were injured.

According to K. K. Dutta, the Santhal revolt had spread in the whole area. The rebels held sway from south-west Taldanga of Birbhumi to Grand Trunk Road and south-east Senathia and Bhagalpur, and from Rajmahal Ganga shore to north-west and north-east of Bhagalpur district. The next target of the rebels was Murshidabad. Many regiments had been stationed on the border of Murshidabad to protect it. Now the Company govt. started having serious perception of these rebels.

On 15th August, 1855, the Company govt. had proclaimed all over the Santhal are a that those Santhals who would want to leave the Santhali rebels and want to come into the service of Company govt. they should go to the nearest English officer and pray for forgiveness and surrender to him. Whoever would do this, his crime would be forgiven. But those who would be on the rebels' side, would be punished.[25]

Although the Company govt. had given an opportunity to the Santhalis to ask for forgiveness, the effect of this proclamation had not been favourable. Those Santhals who were supporters of Siddhu and Kanhu were completely dedicated persons.[26]

The Company govt. knew that the rebels would not be able to withstand its guns and cannons. That is why the big zamindars and Raja had got "towers" built wherever they stayed. There was such a tower built in Pakur. This tower was called "Mortila" tower and was very famous. It was near the bungalow of the Subdivisional officer. This tower was of 20 feet circumference and of 30 feet height. There were 42 holes in the tower alongwith 2 windows. Due to shortage of gunpowder, this tower could not be effective. Siddhu-Kanhu had to face armed soldiers on the banks of the

Terai river. About 200 soldiers drove away 3000 rebels. The Company govt. brought in 14000 soldiers in the Santhal area, and declared "Martial law" on 10 November 1855 which lasted till 2 January 1856.[27]

In this way, the whole area came to be full of soldiers. The soldiers were also acting revengefully. In the confrontation at Maheshpur, Siddhu-Kanhu had also been injured by bullets and they were getting treated at a secret place. The work of the organization was also going on. The soldiers thought that Siddhu-Kanhu must be hiding in Bhognadih so they set fire to it and entirely gutted it. Due to this, Siddhu's father Chunni Manjhi lost his life. Barhait was supposed to be the stronghold of the Santhalis, therefore Barhait was taken under complete control. The officials were enthusiastic to take over complete control over Barhait. Barhait was therefore attacked. In this attack, Chand and Bhairav became martyrs while other braves were killed or captured. But till that time, Siddhu-Kanhu remained beyond the reach of the Govt. Some allurements were offered to capture these 2 leaders.

The Martyrdom of Siddhu-Kanhu

Due to the heavy presence in numbers of the soldiers, the movement was losing steam, but so long as Siddhu and Kanhu were not caught, the movement could not be called dead. During the departure from Maheshpur, the confrontation which took place with the soldiers on the banks of the Terai River, and in which Siddhu and Kanhu got bullet wounds, at that time when they were geeting medical attention in a secret place, the Company govt. in order to catch these leaders was prepared to take any step, hook or by crook. Kanhu got caught in the third week of February in uperbanda which is situated in the north-east of Jamtara. The wharfinger of Kunjra caught Kanhu and handed him over to the English officer Pontet. Similarly, a few days later, Siddhu was arrested in Barhait. Both brothers were hanged on 26th July at Barhait and Bhognadih respectively. Just to terrorise the Santhals, their hanging was carried out at daytime in full view of a crowd of Santhals. The British govt. believed that by instilling fear among the public they could run the administratin peacefully, but this belief was wrong. More important for the govt. was to win the confidence of the Santhals.

The sacrifice of Siddhu-Kanhu and thousands of other Santhals did not remain meaningless. By joining some parts of Birbhumi and some parts of Bhagalpur, a large-spread area of Santhal Parganas was prepared. There were 4 subdistricts of Santhal Parganas-Dumka, Deoghar (alongwith Jamtara), Godda, and Rajmahal (alongwith Pakur). This area of the Santhals was set free from general laws, and for them an Act was implemented in 1855. This Act was the protector of the rights and interests of the Santhals.

List of Reference Books

1. J. B. Bradley Birt , "cry was death to the money lender, the zamindar, the police and all who had taken part or share in the long years of their oppression –The story of Indian Upland, London (1905)," Pg. 189.
2. Ibid. Pg. 189.
3. L. S. S. O. Malley, "District gazetteer Santhal Parganas" second Indian Reprint, New Delhi, Edition 1999, Pg. 23-24.
4. L.S.S.O. Malley, "1790 and 1810 have made their way northwards from Birbhum." Pg. 45.
5. Dr. S. P. Sinha, Santhal Hul, T.R.L. Ranchi, 1992, Pg. 15.
6. L.S.S.O. Malley, quotes Capt. Sherwill, "This valley was a wilderness, inhabited here and there by hill men," the remainder was over run with heavy forest in which wild elephants and tigers were numerous. But in 1851, several hundred substantial Santhal villagers with an abundance of cattle and surrounded by luxuriant crops, occupy this hitherto neglected spot. The hill men have, with a few exception, retired to the hill, op., cit. Pg.45.
7. Dr. S. P. Sinha, Santhal Hul, 1991, Pg. 25
8. L. S. S. O. Malley, "The causes of the rebellion were several, the Santhal themselves declaring their chief grievances were the prevalence of falsehood, the negligence of the sahibs, the extortion of the mahajans, the corruption of the amla, and oppression of the police." Op. cit. Pg. 49-50.
9. W. W. Hunter, Annals of Rural Bengal, London, (1869).
10. Ibid. Pg. 233.
11. Ibid Pg. 229.
12. W. W. Hunter Old Missionary Oxford, 1896, Pg. 69-69
13. A. C. Bidwell, Special Commissioner for suppression of the Santhal Insurrection.
14. A. C. Bidwell to Secretary to the Govt. of Bengal the 18th December, 1855. Bengal W. B. S. A.
15. Ibid.
16. Ibid.
17. Ibid.
18. Ibid.
19. O'Malley, It appears, however, that Khanu and Siddhu proclaimed themselves Lord of the Country under the title of Sabahs and appointed naibs, darogas, and other subordinate officers.
20. K. K. Dutta, "The Santhal Insurrection," Calcutta (1940), Pg. 14-15.
21. Bradley Birt J. B. The story of Indian upland, London (1950) Pg. 189.
22. Karun records, Pancha Kathia record as quoted in Dr. Dutta's Santhal insurrection, Calcutta (1940) Pg. 16.

23. Karun records, Pancha Kathia as quoted, Dr. Dutta's "The Santhals declared their determination to do away with the Bengali and U P country Mahajans, to take possession of the country and set up a government of their own." Santhal insurrection, Calcutta (1940) Pg. 16.
24. K. K. Dutta, op.cit., Pg. 35.
25. The Calcutta Review, Calcutta, 1856.
26. W. W. Hunter, Annals of Rural Bengal, Vol. I, 1868, Pg.249.
27. J. B. Bradley, The story of an Indian upland, London (1905) Pg. 205.

Chapter : Six

Vishwanath Shahdev

("Thakur Vishwanath Shahdev knew that the price of joining the rebels was his "head," but there are some persons who can sacrifice their head for independence. Vishwanath Shahdev was this kind of a warrior.")

Thakur Vishwanath Shahdev

The eastern part of Chhotanagpur Raj was more insecure than the other parts. There used to be sudden attacks from Ramgarh and Singhbhum etc. areas and cattle wealth was driven off or standing crops were cut away. In order to strengthen the eastern area, the then Maharaja Raghunath Shahdev joined Udaipur and Kundu pargana to establish Barkagaon Raj and its responsibility was given to his younger brother Ainee Shah. Thakur Vishwanath Shahdev was of the seventh generation of Ainee Shah. He was born on 12 August 1817. His father's name was Raghunath Shahdev and Mother's name was Baneshwari Kunwar. At proper age Vishwanath Shahdev got married to the sister of Maharaja of Gangpur.

His father Raghunath Shahdev passed away in 1840, so the whole responsibility of the Raj came to rest on the shoulders of Vishwanath Shahdev. Although the 23 year old youth Vishwanath Shahdev knew about affairs of the kingdom, he had more of enthusiasm and less of experience. He made Hatia the capital of his kingdom. Administration could be better managed and was more easy.

Even though Thakur Vishwanath Shahdev was king, the obstructions by the British made him feel crippled. For him, the Christian padres were a problem. Thakur Vishwanath Shahdev despised the tribals who had converted to Christianity. He had observed that the raiyats (farmers) of his Raj had been simple, gentle and well-behaved, but right after conversion to Christianity they used to become impertinent and indisciplined. They used to think that by adopting the religion of the British they had become equal to the British. The Raja or the zamindar had no importance with them. The behaviour of the converted tribals could never be tolerated by Vishwanath Shahdev. He had banned the entry of Christian padres with in the boundaries of his Raj. The raiyats of Vishwanath Shahdev used to give him full respect. Shahdev also had full confidence on his subjects.

In Chhotanagpur, traditionally there were some customs which were easily ignored by the British Govt. In Doranda, there was land of Barkaraj and if here the military cantonment was set up by the British then why was the permission of the Raj not taken to use this land ? Similarly, with whose orders the German Christian padres were settling and spreading ? Vishwanath Shahdev wrote a complaint appeal to the Lt. Governor of Bengal Mr. Halliday on 15 August 1856 that the converted Christians have spread terror in his Raj. They are settling down near Doranda and spreading, without his permission.[1]

Partiality and Injustice

Due to underhand agreement between missionaries and Govt. officers, Thakur Vishwanath Shahdev was enduring the sting of partiality and injustice. The German padres were working behind three converted kols who submitted 3 separate prayers to the District officer J. N. Davis's court. They were heard and judgement was passed on 28 February 1856. It was nearly certain that the decision would be in favouur of the 3 Kol converts. This would give strength to religious expansion. Vishwanath Shahdev and his men were found guilty of sabotage and attacking the converted Kols. Vishwanath Shahdev was slapped with a fine of Rs.200/-, his man with Rs.100/-, and the other saboteurs were fined at the rate of Rs.50, per head. The total amount of the fine was Rs.2297.8.[2]

The sentence was appealed against in the court of the Judicial Commissioner W. H. Oakes. The Judicial Commissioner did not put any effort to go to the root and facts of the case, so the order of the lower court was upheld and the appeal of Vishwanath Shahdev was dismissed. Dis-satisfied, Vishwanath Shahdev knocked on the doors of the Sadar nizamat Adalat. If defeat was accepted then the rights of all zamindars would be violated and the missionaries with renewed vigour world start showing the zamindars in a poor light. Actually this case was against the illegal capture by the missionaries of the traditional rights of the Rajas and zamindars. The question was not only that of fine and Vishwanath Shahdev. The decision of the case affected all the zamindars.

The sadar Nizamat Adalat did not find any legal flaw in the case. It was based on the evidence of witnesses and eyewitnesses. Hence sadar nizamal Adalat returned the case "as it is." There was no other court available hence appeal to the Lt. Governor was the only alternative left. Thus Pitambar Singh and Lalit Rai came forward as Manager of Barkagaon raj and they filed an appeal on 16 August, 1856 to the Lt. Governor F. D. Halliday and tried to focus his attention on this partiality which the British officers always had for the Christian missionaries.[3] Justice had been sold in the name of religion.

In the appeal, mention was made of one Raja Lal Loknath Shahi whom the Govt. had promoted as sub. Asstt. Commissioner because he used always to take the side of British officers and Christian Padres.

In another appeal filed by Kanhai Ram Tiwari on 23 July 1856 complaint was made about the newly converted Kols who thereafter took possession of lands by force. The German mission padres used to present the case of the converted kols and the court used to listen to them. Decision used to be in their favour. It had also been said in the appeal petition that if such kind of favouritism kept on continuing then within a short time half of Nagpur would become Christian and there would be no land left for agriculture.

The Lt. Governor of Bengal Mr. F. D. Halliday handed over all the appeals to Chhotanagpur Commissioner Allen and gave him the responsibility to give his suggestions. Allen had a fixed notion that Vishwanath Shahdev and his officials were very uppity in their behavior.[4] Later all the appeals were rejected.

With the rejection of his appeal Thakur Vishwanath Shahdev became very sad internally. He felt that to hope for justice from this govt. was meaningless. This govt. belongs to Christian missionaries and sycophants. The lower or district level govt. employees were in favour of the missionaries. Even the officers of the central level were not in favour of doing justice. Thakur Vishwanath Shahdev began thinking of probability of getting an opportunity to free the country of the British govt.

Vishwanath Shahdev Chief

Vishwanath Shahdev was elected as the chief of the freedom fighters. Vishwanath Shahdev had known Madho Singh leader of the Ramgarhia soldiers and Nadir Ali Khan from before. Vishwanath Shahdev had suggested to them to revolt on 23 June because 23 June was the day of Rathyatra, but at that time the soldier leaders could not come to a consensus. Apart from

Madho Singh, Nadir Ali, leaders of the soldiers, Jaimangal Pandey, who was the leader of the soldiers of Doranda cantonment, was very experienced.

According to the soldier leaders, so long as a chief and a commander are not appointed, a well-knit organization of the soldiers could not be developed. At first the soldier leaders tried for the joining of Maharaja Jagannath Shahi of Nagpur with them, but the Maharaja thought it to be beneficial to remain aloof from the rebels. Davis had given to Dalton the information about Maharaja Jagannath not having any concern with the rebels.[5] Thereafter the soldiers talked to Upendra Nath Shahi, nephew of the Maharaja and heir apparent but he, too, did not want to join the soldiers. Under the circumstances, for Vishwanath Shahdev to fearlessly go ahead and take over the responsibility of "chief" was brave work. Due to this the soldiers could not be scattered, nor was the scattering allowed to come. Pandey Ganpat Rai, by taking over the responsibility of Commander of the army, gave an organized look to the soldiers' organization.

Thakur Vishwanath Shahdev set up his office in a vacant bungalow at Doranda and regularly held "Kutcherry." An individual has some blunt or harsh attitudes. Thakur Vishwanath Shahdev could not tolerate Christian padres as also converted Kols. He knew that the Christian converted Kol would always work against the soldier govt. Hence it was necessary to crush them. Additionally, some zamindars and kings had been tortured by the British. They were also the victims of favouritism. Thus it was a good opportunity that all the people victimized by the British be brought on a common platform. The important people who were victims of atrocities of the British and who lived near Nagpur were the following :

1. Raja Neelmani Singhdeo – Raja of Panchet
2. Arjun singh – Raja of Singhbhum. The British used to try for his downfall and encouraged his co-sharers, the Rajas of Kharsawan etc. to come up.
3. Bhawani Buksh Rai – zamindar, Palamau.
4. Nilambar and Pitambar Shahi - Palamau. All of them were happy with the sipahi mutiny, and all wanted to free the country from the clutches of the British.

The suggestion of Thakur Vishwanath Shahdev was very good except that there was no effort to bring the aforementioned powers on a common platform. There were many problems for the Royal govt. of Thakur. Despite all those, there was a need for an information department for the Royal govt. to win the confidence of the public. Zamindar Kurban Ali was appointed to do this work, and to assist him Bal Govind Shahi and Nathi

Khan were appointed. Kurban Ali started the work of "propaganda" on 4 August.

Hazaribagh and Pithoria

First of all, Thakur Vishwanath Shahdev wanted to destroy and take over possession of all those areas where they were loyal to the British and doing their work. Amongst the traitors of the country, Ramgarh's Shambhunath Singh and Pithoria's zamindar Jagatpal Singh were chief ones. Both these places were at the borders of Ranchi. Hazaribgh's capital Ichak was a safe place, and for Dalton, etc it was considered to be trustworthy hiding place. Pithoria Jagatpal Singh was engaged in sending information about the soldier's govt. to Dalton. The cooperation of the Raja of Hazaribagh and zamindar of Pithoria was very useful in the return of Dalton.

The soldiers of the Doranda cantonment were divided in 3 parts – Ramgarhia sainik, |Bhagalpuria and Hindustani sainik. One had to work with patience and comprehension to satisfy and keep them together. Thakur Vishwanath Shahdev was supposed to be close to the Ramgarhia Sainiks. All the soldiers had accepted the proposal to attack Hazaribagh.

The role of the Chutu Palu Raj was important for the travel from Ranchi to Hazaribagh. Although Ormanjhi was next to Ramgarh Raj but despite keeping his capital at Ormanjhi, Tikait Umrao Singh was against British rule. He sent a message to Thakur Vishwanath Shahdev that in the event of attack on Hazaribagh he would give his full cooperation.

The Crown of Thorns

In the beginning although it appeared to be easy, the chair of the Chief however was equally complicated. Difference in opinion about the next step to be taken by the soldiers came to the fore. Due to difference in opinion in the 3 parts of the soldiers, indiscipline started creeping in among them. Bhagalpuria Jaimangal Pandey's proposal was that they should gain victory over Calcutta. They should first go to Singhbhum, not Doranda, from where after getting the soldiers freed they should increase their strength. In the meantime the soldiers of Sambalpur should be freed to capture Midnapur and establish themselves. Thereafter the next target would have to be Calcutta. In the contemporary circumstances, Calcutta's importance was more than of Delhi.

Opposite to Jai Mangal Pandey, Madho Singh thought it right to at first meet Babu Kunwar Singh. This was an important problem, to solve which, a meeting was called at Parade Ground.

The meeting started under the Chairmanship of Thakur Vishwanath Shahdev. There was no shortage of speakers. Indiscipline was at its height. Ultimately it was decided that meeting Babu Kunwar Singh would be appropriate. In the name of unity of soldiers, Madho Singh could get Jai Mangal Pandey over to his side. The dignity and awe of Thakur Vishwanath Shahdev was torn to shreds. The soldiers Achraj Singh, Pahalwan Singh, Kawwab Ali Khan not only showed disdain to Thakur Vishwanath but also threatened to decapitate him. Thakur Vishwanath Shahdev was not ready to endure such indiscipline, hence along with his Hatia supporters came out of the meeting.

After this incident, Thakur Vishwanath Shahdev could not be seen in Doranda Cantonment. He found these soldier-leaders to be equally despotic as "Oakes and Davis." Mentally he was perplexed. He had put his trust opposite to Dalton and now it was not possible to come back. Vishwanath Shahdev discussed the matter with Maharaja of Chhotanagpur Jagannath Shahi. He also contacted Pithoria's Jagatpal Singh. He expressed his disgust against the soldiers.[6] The feeling to be freed from British rule was a part of his nature, hence he was by nature a rebel. Maharaja Jagannath Shahi or Jagatpal Singh of Pithoria were men of the British. It does not seem to be possible that Thakur Vishwanath Shahdev would have taken steps to contact Jagatpal. The Raja of Chhotanagpur Jagannath Shahi was in favour of the British on this matter. He never went against the British openly. He helped the British to crush the movement as and when required.[7] Under the circumstances, Dalton note on this matter was an effort to ruin the image of Vishwanath Shahdev. It was correct that the assemblage of soldiers at Doranda had different opinions, but on one point everybody was of the same opinion that it was not possible to stay cut off from the other rebel soldiers of the country.

And again, the British were not sitting quietly. They had full confidence on Sikh soldiers and they had no dearth of resources. As per requirement, they were recruiting soldiers. Under the British, the soldiers were only to obey orders, policy decision was the work of army officials. There was a lack of consensus among the soldier-leaders of Doranda. Soldiers are meant only for blind obedience of orders, but such discipline was not remaining among the Doranda soldiers. This had become clear on the parade ground meeting, yet a consensus had evolved to go and meet Babu Kunwar Singh.

There was a difference in opinion between Madho Singh and "Thakur Vishwanath Shahdev about the timing of leaving Doranda. Vishwanath Shahdev wanted to go in October after Dusschra, but Madho Singh thought that enough delay had taken place. The British will not remain quiet. Delay may prove to be fatal. Vishwanath Shahdev appreciated the experience of Madho Singh, so on 10 September the soldiers started for Rohtasgarh. Commissioner E.T.Dalton had written in his letter dated 14 September that the rebel soldiers had terrorized Ranchi city by looting and plundering.[8]

The number of soldiers-freedom fighters of Doranda was about 600, and in their weaponry they had 4 cannons from which 6 pounder balls could be fired. After crossing the Tiku Ghat, it took 2 days to cover the 10 mile route to Balumath. The Balumath Mahant had been given prior information and message that he should collect enough rations, and donations from the traders and be ready.

Betrayal by the Mahant

Thakur Vishwanath Shahdev was greatly shocked by the behavior of the Mahant. The Mahant disappeared 2 days prior to the arrival of the soldiers. He had said while leaving that he was going out to collect donations. This was a sever blow which badly affected the soldiers. The traders of Chatra also did not cooperate whereas Major English who had been staying at Chatra alongwith his troops was assured of rations and other facilities. Just like the Mahant of Balumath, the Chatra traders also did not cooperate.

In the meantime, the Chatra traders had received the information that the British had again taken over the Doranda Cantonment. This information influenced the trading class, while it destroyed the morale of the freedom fighters.

In order to overcome the monetary problem, Thakur Vishwanath Shahdev wanted to return to Hatia, but in the third week of September, circumstances were rapidly changing in favour of the British. Dalton had re-occupied Doranda cantonment and this he thought was a psychological victory among the public.

The freedom fighters were being surrounded with difficulties. They went from Balumath to Chatra. There was no arrangement for food. Madho Singh along with some soldiers, could not collect adequate donations from Chatra's businessmen who had already obtained information of the coming of the British troops. On 2 October, armed with Enfield rifles, the British troops tried to surround the freedom fighters. During those times Enfield guns were supposed to be the best. Its target range was 900 yards.[9] On the morning of 2 October, the troops of Major English surrounded the freedom fighters. If there had been a frontal attack then the cannons would have been useful. Major English's troops were in a mango orchard and firing from behind the trees. For some time the fight continued but gradually the number of freedom fighters lessened. Simpson, in a letter, acknowledged the benefit of the mango trees.[10] The District Officer Hazaribagh, Simpson, reported to Govt. about the fight with the Doranda rebel soldiers who could not withstand Simpson's troops. His troops could lay their hands on 4 cannons as well as enough ammunition and guns of the rebel soldiers.[11] Along with Jaimangal Pandey, hundreds of prisoners of war were hanged from trees. Their cases were heard under Act XVII, 1857.

Thakur Vishwanath Shahdev and Pandey Ganpat Rai were boosting the morale of the fighting soldiers. They had no knowledge of war-skills. Seeing the dispersal of the Doranda soldiers, they thought it appropriate to return to Ranchi or Lohardaga. On 3 October, the palanquin of Vishwanath Shahdev was found in the jungle and his 2palanquin bearers-cum-servants were captured. It comes to light from the statements of these 2 palanquin bearers that during the battle Thakur Vishwanath Shahdev and Pandey Ganpat Rai had been staying with the soldiers.[12]

According to the palanquin bearers, in order to escape capture by the enemy, Thakur Vishwanath Shahdev and Pandey Ganpat Rai, taking cover of the night, had proceeded towards Ranchi. Thakur Vishwanath Shahdev had wanted to raise near Lohardaga an intercepting army.[13] In this work he got the support of Bahorun Singh, a released from jail convict who had himself raised a troop of 200 trained soldiers.

The revolution of the masses in 1854, although it was officially termed by the govt. as "sepoy-mutiny" but in a practical form, it was indeed a people's revolution. When the Doranda soldiers requested the Maharaja, his nephew and other family members to lead them, their request was not accepted. Finally, Thakur Vishwanath Shahdev took up the responsibility of leading them. The soldiers started to go to Babu Kunwar Singh and meet him. The soldiers committed 2 mistakes which were rued by all : (i) they should have taken the Palamau route to reach Babu Kunwar Singh instead of Chatra, and (2) Trusting the traders of Chatra. Before Thakur Vishwanath Shahdev could arrange for rations, the British troops attacked them. Under the circumstances it was expected that the soldiers would runaway from the battlefield.

Col. E. T. Dalton believed in terrorizing the minds of the Hindustanis to such an extent that for the next 200 years no Hindustani would have the courage to raise his head against the British Govt. Influenced by this aim, the British started hanging people publicly.[14] Along with this, the work of searching out the rebels was taken up on a war footing. Prize money/rewards were also proclaimed. This truth is undeniable that the continued existence of the British Raj in India was due to the important role played by traitors.

Thakur Vishwanath Shahdev also fell victim to treachery. A person called Vishwanath Dubey passed on information to the British govt. due to which Vishwanath Shahdev was caught. The following charges were framed against Vishwanath Shahdev :

(1) Siding with the rebel soldiers of Ramgarh.

(2) Obstructing the mountain routes due to which Govt. officials could not reach Ranchi.

(3) Promising to give kingly pay to the soldiers thus agitating them.

(4) Collecting Rs. 25000/- from the businessmen by force.

Thakur Vishwanath Shahdev was brought before the court of the Judicial Commissioner. As per apprehension, death sentence in the form of hanging, was handed over to him. The present Shaheed Chowk on which stood a branch of the kadamba tree, Thakur Vishwanath Shahdev's life was snuffed out by hanging him from it. By becoming a martyr, Thakur Vishwanath Shahdev became immortal in the history of Jharkhand. Friday, 16 April is the date of his immortality.[15] The British had a feeling that by carrying out hanging in front of a crowd, the people would be terrorized. In their British heads this thought did not occur that in some youths in the crowd, the desire for martyrdom would awake.

The punishment for freedom was not limited to only hanging. The Commissioner of Chhotanagpur wrote to Bengal Govt. to seize all the properties of Vishwanath Shahdev.[16] As per suggestion of the Commissioner, all 97 villages of Barkagaon and the property of the Jagannathpur Mandir were seized in December 1857.[17] Over a period of time the property written in the name of Jagannathpur Mandir was returned to the priest by Bengal Govt.

The whole family of Vishwanath Shahdev scattered. Wife Thakurani Waneshwari Kumari was not able to endure the hanging of her husband so she went and settled in village Khora, district Gumla, along with her only son Kapil Nath Shahdev. She had left Ranchi a few days prior to the hanging. 14 years of her life in Khora village was a period of austerity. She took the advice of lawyers and in 1842 filed a case in Calcutta High Court praying for return of Barkagarh Raj. In the case, mention had been made of the rules of the Mitakshara Law of Inheritance. But the Court ruled in favour of British govt. It was also said in the judgement that in case of special dispute the zamindari would go back to the original Raja. In this case Maharaja Jagannath Shahi speaking in favour of Kapilnath Shahi had stated that the zamindari was "Khorpos" in nature and given as a means of livelihood. The troubles of the Thakurani increased after losing the case.

After the revolt, soldiers of various orgins had come together in the Doranda cantonment. Three origins were clear-Ramgarhia, Darbhangiya and Hindustani, and every origin had separate commanders. Above them a commander-in-chief, and a "chief" or Raja was necessary otherwise the soldiers would scatter. The rebel soldiers at first had contacted Maharaja Jagannath Shahi. After he refused, his heir Udai Narain Shahi, and the zamindars who were directly related to the Maharaja were also contacted but none wanted to join them. Thakur Vishwanath Shahdev came forward and took up the responsibility, and an organized appearance of the soldiers took shape. Thakur Vishwanath Shahdev knew that the price of joining the freedom fighters was his head but there are some people who for the sake of independence do not shy away from sacrificing their heads. Thakur Vishwanath Shahdev was also such a warrior. When big zamindars and Rajas were ignoring the rebel soldiers, then at that time Thakur Vishwanath Shahdev came forward and lighted the torch of leading the soldiers.

List of Reference Books

1. Petition of Thakur Vishwanath Shahdev, Malik of Barkagarh in Chhotanagpur, at 15 Aug. 1856, Bengal (crim.) proceed. No.238, dt. 11 Sept. 1856.
2. P. Kumar, Mutinies and Rebellions in Chhotanagpur, Delhi, 1991, Pg. 99.
3. Petition of Pitambar Singh etc. dt.16 Aug. 1856. Beng. Judl (crim) proceed no. 239, dt. 11 sept. 1856.
4. Thakur Bishwanath Shahi was generally not well spoken of in his neighbourhood. Extract from the letter Allen to C. T. Backland Junior secy. 22 Dec. 1856, Beng. Judl (crim), proceed no. 248, dt. 15 January, 1857.
5. J. S. Davis District officer to E. T. Dalton dt. 27 October, 1857, Lohardagga Des. Vol. no. 73
6. Dalton Young, Hazaribagh dt. 5 Sept. 1857. Home (pub.) cons. No. 26, dt. 18 Sept. 1857.
7. Ranchi Gazetteer : "The Maharaja and other important zamindars, however, helped the British authorities to crush the movement." P. 58.
8. Dalton to Young : ".... The mutinous sepoys are all said to have behaved in the most brutal manner to the townspeople, plundering, torturing and violating their women" 14 Sept. 1857, Home (bub.) cons. No. 94 dt. 25 Sept. 1857.
9. P. C. Roy Choudhary 1857 in Bihar (Chhotanagpur and Santhal Pargana) Patna 1957 Pg. 41
10. Simpson to Dalton, "Had there not been the trees to afford parties cover to them, the loss on their side must have been greater...." Kali Pahar Chatra, dt. 4 October, 1857, Home (pub.) con. No.107, dt. 10 Oct. 1857.

11. Simpson to Secy. Govt. of Bengal dt. 4 Oct. 1857. Home (Pub.) Cons No.107 dt. 30 October, 1857
12. The letter written by Simpson to Dalton dt. 4 Oct. 1857. Extract P. C. Rai, Pg. Home (pub.) con. No.107,
13. R. G. "Thakur Bishwanath returned to Chhotanagpur and organized a resistance movement against the British in the neighbourhood of Lohardagga" pg. 69.
14. Ranchi Gazetteer, Pg. 60
15. Ibid. Pg. 60.
16. Commissioner Chhotanagpur to Secy. Govt. of Bengal, Letter no.9 dt. 4 Oct. 1858 Ibid to 61 F. N.
17. R. G. Pg. 61.

Chapter : Seven

Pandey Ganpat Rai

("Persons take birth and thereafter they pass away, but their thoughts and ideals do not pass away. Pandeya Ganpat Rai, by becoming a martyr, lit such a torch that till date the earth of this place remains lighted by it.")

Pandeya Ganpat Rai

Amongst the martyrs of Jharkhand, the name of Pandeya Ganpat Rai is taken very respectfully. Pandeya Ganpat Rai was very intelligent and lively right from childhood. He was born in Bhowro, a village in Lohardagga, on 17 January 1809. From childhood he had an interest in warfare, and as a young boy he became quite proficient in swordsmanship. Since the village was situated amidst jungles, it was a routine matter to go inside the jungles. His uncle Sadashiv Rai was the divan (court minister) of the Chhotanagpur Maharaja, and used to stay at Palkot. Boy Ganpat Rai was sent to stay under the protection of his uncle.

During those days, Palkot was the capital of Chhotanagpur. There was no dearth of learned scholars in the Raja's court. Learned scholars of Sanskrit and Maulvis of Arabi and Farsi were available in Palkot. Ganpat Rai studied the state language "Nagpuri" as also Arabi and Farsi. His sharp intellect and ability to debate were second to none. Staying at Palkot Ganpat Rai learnt a lot of courtly behavior from the Raj durbar.

People had praised a lot regarding debating prowers and sharp intellect of Ganpat Rai. The incident goes like this- Ganpat Rai, accompanied by his uncle had once gone with a bridegroom's party. In those days the custom was that there would be sword play between the bride's party and the bridegroom's party. People nominated Ganpat Rai as the representative of the bridegroom's party. The 15 year old Ganpat Rai astounded the bride's party and that is how the bridegroom's party became victorious.[1]

Attracted by the keen prowess of Pandeya Ganpat Rai, a marriage proposal for him was then and there placed before his uncle. He gave his consent upon which that very day, his engagement took place followed by his marriage under the same marriage canopy. Thus, Ganpat Rai who had come as a member of the groom's party, returned as a groom alongwith his bride.

He had no children from this wife. Hence, upon the pleading of the first wife, his family members got him married again. Sugandh Kunwar, daughter of Mohan Sinha of Bangladih Karar, district Palamau, became his second wife. She gave birth to 2 sons and 3 daughters. After the passing away of his uncle Sadashiv Rai, Ganpat Rai was appointed Diwan of the Maharaja of Chhotanagpur. He was well versed in the Court practices and regulations. Due to becoming Diwan, it became necessary for him to stay at Palkot, hence most of his time was spent in Palkot. Ganpat Rai became quite famous as a diwan but in proportion to his fame, the number of jealous people began to increase. Ganpat Rai was normally a simple and large-hearted Diwan.

In those days, Chhotanagpur Raj was fighting a legal battle on the question of "successor." The case went up to the Privy Council but the decision went against the Nagvanshi Raja. Due to this legal battle, the life of Maharaja Jagannath Shahdev became endangered. For his protection, he was brought to Bhowro, the birth place of Ganpat Rai, so, Bhowro developed in the form of the capital of the Raj. In 1870 the British govt. appointed Adam Hume, Administrator of Chhotanagpur Raj in order to run the Raj. In this way, openly the British Administrators established their right over Chhotanagpur. Pandey Ganpat Rai, too, was very angry at this incident.[2]

Ganpat Rai and the treachery of Nagpur Raj :

Living among the tribes, Ganpat Rai lacked practicality in his mentol development. During such kind of mental tension, Pandeya Ganpat Rai received the news that Bahadur Shah Jafar was still the real Emperor (Badshah). Ganpat Rai's emotions reached sky high.[3] Ganpat Rai thought that Bahadur Shah Jafar would help him. The whole strength lay in Delhi. The politics of the country is controlled by Delhi. In the mind of Pandeya Ganpat Rai, the throne of Nagpur Raj started shining. The way Durjansaal had obtained "firman" or order from Shahenshah Jahangir to become a king, somewhat like that a "firman" could be got issued by showing such a big military strength. Pandey Ganpat Rai had a meeting with Madho Singh, Jaimangal Pandey and a few other soldier leaders. Ganpath Rai successfully convinced the leaders that at that time the whole fight was divided in 2 camps Shah Alam versus British. They should support the Emperor. For that it was necessary to meet Vir Kunwar Singh.

According to the additional plan of Ganpat Rai, first of all it was essential to meet Kunwer Singh. Thakur Vishwanath Shahdev alongwith most of the people had a consensus that first of all it would be appropriate to go to Kunwar Singh. Since this decision was convenient for his plan, Ganpat Rai had remained silent. Ultimately, every one agreed that the next place of halt would be Jagdishpur.

Problem of Supply

The problem of supplying ammunitions, some labourers and food for the soldiers was staring in the face and no body was coming forward. Some soldier leaders suggested over-running the Raja of Hazaribagh so that immediately the financial problem could be solved. Finding the circumstances changing, Pandey Ganpat Rai had to come forward. Although the soldiers in Doranda had been divided in 3 parts and a common decision had not emerged as to which day and in which direction to go, it was not good to delay any further. Hence Madho Singh decided to leave for Rohtasgarh on Sunday 2 September, 1857. Before Col. Fisher could come with his troops, they would have to leave Doranda. Pandeya Ganpat Rai was asked to supply coolies, labourers and other resources. Pandeya Ganpat Rai informed the Maharaja of Nagpur that he had been selected to command the rebel troops, and the rebel soldiers would need for a while 10,000 coolies and labourers for their next programme.[4] But it was not an easy task to provide 10,000 coolies and labourers. Jaimangal Pandey, who was an experienced soldier, and had worked with Major Russage and Wilkinson, said that joint efforts would have to be made by Thakur Vishwanath Shahdev, Govind Shahi, Ganpat Rai and others to overcome this problem.[5]

Pandey Ganpat Rai had calculated that being the commander of the rebel army would be a great power and Maharaja Jagannath Shahi out of sheer fright of this power would manage the supply. But, just the reverse happened- his letter reached E. T. Dalton. The Maharaja's relation with Pandey Ganpat Rai was not cordial Ganpat Rai had left Doranda and moved with the rebel soldiers on Friday 11 Sept. 1857 towards Rohtasgarh. The soldiers were about 600 in number. Apart from old guns some small and big cannons were also with them. The soldiers crossed Tiku Ghat and marched forward. Their biggest problem was lack of funds and lack of adequate supplies. Pandeya Ganpat Rai had sent requests for cooperation to the Mahant of Balumath and traders of Chatra, but they betrayed the freedom fighters.

Major English had reached Chatra with a troop comprising of Sikhs and Madrasis. The freedom fighters had not been prepared for them. Suddenly both the troops clashed. On 3 October Major English sent message of victory through telegram and informed that 4 cannons along with ammunitions were recovered. There were 45 casualties from his side for which Major English made a further demand of 100 soldiers.[6] The defeat and scattering of the Doranda freedom fighters was unfortunate, and the reason was the non-cooperation of the public and traders. In order to get adequate rations, the freedom fighters had to loot and plunder while crossing the Tiku Ghat.

Hence they suffered loss of image with the public. If the Balumath Mahant and the traders of Chatra had cooperated, then they would have been certainly victorious.[7] On the other hand, Major English did not have any problem regarding adequate supplies. The defeat at Chatra resulted in the scattering of the rebel troops.

Under cover of darkness, Thakur Vishwanath Shahdev and Pandey Ganpat Rai could go and hide in a safe place. The arrested about 150 freedom fighting troops were executed by hanging from trees lining the Harijeewan pond. Jaimangal Pandey and Nadir Ali had been hanged on the bank of this pond which is now famous as "Phansi Talab."

Unaffected by the defeat at Chatra, Thakur Vishwanath Shahdev and Pandey Ganpat Rai once again bused themselves in organization work. Now it was a difficult job because both Vishwanath Shahdev and Ganpat Rai had come in the focus of the British govt. which was trying to arrest them. Ganpat Rai hid for a few days in his own village Bhowro the news of which reached Major Nation. The Major took a band of 100 soldiers and reached Bhowro village and laid siege to it. This was a difficult situation. But Ganpat Rai was no less. He wrapped himself in a blanket, dressed up as a shepherd, and very soon through deceiving Major Nation, he escaped from his grip.

Pandey Ganpat Rai was very popular in his area but had equal number of enemies as well. Right from the court of the Maharaja to small and big zamindars there were enemies. Vishwanath Shahdev was the chief of the soldiers of Doranda cantonment while Pande Ganpat Rai was the commander. As commander, Pandeya Ganpat Rai had asked the Maharaja for 10,000 labourers to work as coolies but the Maharaja did not give in to his pressure, so Vishwanath Shahdev had to go in for alternative arrangement.

Pandeya Ganpat Rai was an enthusiastic person and was supposed to be well-versed in the formulation of policies. If the soldiers of Doranda believed Vishwanath Shahdev as Shakti or strength, they believed Ganpat Rai to be their wisdom. His advice or suggestions were given importance. Pandeya Ganpat Rai however could not bring the supply he had promised, due to which Vishwanath Shahdev had to take help from the Hatiya residents. Ganpat Rai firmly believed that due to the opposition of the Maharaja he could not fulfill the pledge he had given. He was of the opinion that first of all, Raja Shambhu Nath Singh of Hazaribagh which was the place of refuge for the British, should be taken over and thereafter the next step should be taken. The later on incidents proved how correct was the opinion of Ganpat Rai. The role of Hazaribagh in the return of the British to Ranchi was very important. Everybody wanted to reach Babu Kunwar Singh at the earliest but scattered after reaching Chatra. Major English reached Chatra with his mostly Sikh troops, and the rebel troops fighting hunger for the past 2 days had not been able to normalize, when on 1 October troops of both sides clashed. As expected, the freedom fighters of Doranda cantonment could not withstand the troops of Major English. Some were killed, some escaped at the first opportunity and some fell wounded who were hanged the next day.

Thereafter Bhowro village could not continue to be a safe place for Pandeya Ganpat Rai so he had to look for another safe place. At night itself, he alongwith his priest Udainath Pathak had to leave for Lohardagga. Just to spend the night he wanted to go to an old and very trust worthy friend who used to stay in Cambo village. But due to bad luck, being unable to make out the correct route at night, he reached Parhepat and not Cambo village. The zamindar of Parhepat was Mahesh Shahi who was on the side of the British. Mahesh Shahi was very pleased and welcomed Ganpat Rai but at the same time sent information to Lohardagga. Not knowing the treacherous nature of Mahesh Shahi, Ganapat Rai thought it appropriate to spend the night there. Mahesh Shahi bolted his door from outside at an opportune moment.

Early in the morning Major Nation and some soldiers reached from Lohardagga and surrounded the house of Mahesh Shahi. Major Nation got the room opened and thereafter he arrested Ganpat Rai. A freedom fighter of the land of Nagpur fell victim to treachery.

Pandeya Ganpat Rai was produced before Commissioner E. T. Dalton on 21 April 1858 and as had been decided from before, Pandeya Ganpat Rai was awarded sentence of death by hanging. The officials had been ready from before. In Shaheed Chowk from the same branch of the Kadamba tree which had been used for hanging Thakur Vishwanath Shahdev on 16 April, Pandeya Ganpat "Rai was hanged to death on 21 April.

Persons are born and they die too, but their thoughts and ideals do not die. Pandeya Ganpat Rai by becoming a martyr lit such a light of freedom that even now this land of Nagpur stands illumined.

List of Reference books

1. Bihar District Gazetteer Ranchi, Patna, 1970, Pg. 58
2. Secy. To Govt. of Bengal to Secy. Govt. of India, no : 849 dt. 20 March 1858, For sec. cons. No.358
3. P. Kumar, "when he heard the news of the coup of Hazaribagh and Ranchi, and that Bahadur Shah was now again the defacto Emperor of India, all these events with a vast opportunity fired his imagination"- Mutinees and Rebellions in Chhotanagpur Delhi, 1991, Pg. 185
4. Col. Dalton quotes the letter of Pandeya Ganpat Rai to Maharaja Chhotanagpur in his letter to Davis no. 58, Dated 5 October, 1857, Chhotanagpur Commer's Des. Vol. 214.
5. Evidence of Jaimangal Pandey at Chatra on 4th October, 1857, Dalton's to Young, no.: 61, dt. 23 Oct. 1857, Chhotanagpur Commer's Des. Vol. 218.
6. P. C. Roy Choudhary 1857 in Bihar, Stanfon to Secy. Govt. of India. Transmitted the message of Major English from Sherghati Electric Telegraph Office to Calcutta on 3rd. Oct. 1857.
7. R. G., "The tragic lack of intelligence regarding the movement of enemy and the treachery of the Mahajan of Chatra cost them their victory." Pg. 59.

Chapter : Eight

Tikait Umrao Singh

(Charu-Chutupalu (Ramgarh Ghat) Route Cannot be used by any foreign troops to go to Ranchi)

Tikait Umrao Singh

The freedom spark which ignited on 10 May, 1857 in the Army Cantonment of Meerut did not take much time in spreading all over the country. By the last week of July, a wave of dis-satisfaction was palpable in Hazaribagh Army Cantonment so much so that at any moment the soldiers could revolt. Sitting at Ranchi, the Commissioner Chhotanagpur Col. E. T. Dalton and other officers were discussing about the then Army problems. Ultimately it was decided to send Lt. Graham along with troops under him to Hazaribagh, disarm the soldiers there and put by their arms and ammunition. Graham started with 2 companies of soldiers, 30 cavalrymen and 2 cannons on the 1st. of August for Hazaribagh. After having covered some distance, he got the information that the soldiers of Hazaribagh had revolted.[1]

This news proved explosive for Lt. Graham Leaving the cavalrymen, the soldiers and the gunners along with cannons and elephants he immediately returned to Doranda. The soldiers were under the leadership of jamadar Madho Singh, and Nadir Ali had taken over the responsibility of the cannons. When Madho Singh reached Ormanjhi after crossing the mountainous road, he met Tikait Umrao Singh and his supporters. Tikait Umrao Singh informed Madho Singh that the mountain road will be prohibited for use by European soldiers.[2] A crowd had collected in Ormanjhi to have a look at the freedom fighters.

Tikait Umraao Singh was born in village Khatanga of Ormanjhi block. Right from childhood he had been rebellious in nature. Having the courage to die for his ideals, young Umrao Singh never married-rather, he dedicated his full time for the good of his country and subjects. Tikait Umrao Singh had a zamindari of 12 villages, namely, (i) Khatanga (ii) Harchanda (iii) Jhiri (iv) Dahu (v) Barwe (vi) Bartuli (vii) Hesatu (viii) Kutey (ix) Gagarii (x) Sildiri (xi) Kuwalu and (xii) Chapawight. The mountain route under his jurisdiction was Chutupalu to Charu. From the military point of view the jurisdiction area of Tikait Umrao Singh was of great importance.

The Importance of the mountain road

The mountain road which was under the authority and jurisdiction of Tikait Umrao Singh connected Ranchi to Hazaribagh. If from Hazaribagh one goes to Ranchi then after Ramgarh the climb of the mountain road starts. On the right hand side there are high mountains and on the left hand side is a deep valley and amidst these 2 sides there is a narrow path which climbs up. Due to slightest negligence one can fall hundreds of feet below. But apart from this route there is another road from Hazaribagh which is very tortuous and takes a lot of time. This was the reason why the mountain road in Umrao Singh's authority was preferred by the traders and soldiers. Tikait Umrao Singh was the keeper of this pass.

Keeping in mind the importance of this pass, every side wanted to include Tikait Umrao Singh on their side. The British, who were fighting for their existence, gave a lot of importance to the safety of this route. If this route is cut off at places then it would be impossible to cross the route. For this reason Col. E. T. Dalton had issued a warning letter to Tikait Umrao Singh saying that if the mountain road was damaged or cut then the whole responsibility would devolve on him and for which he could be sentenced to death.[3]

Tikait and the Raja of Hazaribagh

The Raja of Hazaribagh Shambhunath Singh and Tikait Umrao Singh were always at loggerheads. Both were sworn enemies of each other. During the time of Sepoy Mutiny, the loyalty of Raja Shambhunath Singh towards the British was at the highest level. The doors of the Raj Mahal were open to the British during any sudden misfortune. Opposite to him was Tikait Umrao Singh who favoured the independence of the country. He wanted that Thakur Vishwanath Shahdev should attack Hazaribagh and occupy it. There were 2 benefits to be seen clearly : (1) The connectivity of the British from Hazaribagh to Ranchi would end and (2) A suspicion that European soldiers would reach Ranchi Via the Hazaribagh and Ramgarh mountain pass, would prove to be just a rumour. Thakur Vishwanath Shahdev and the Ramgarhi soldiers were in favour of attacking Hazaribagh soon otherwise due to Hazaribagh it would become easier for the European troops to enter Nagpur.

In this context, Tikait Umrao Singh gave full support to Thakur Vishwanath Shahdev. Tikait Umrao Singh thought the Raja of Hazaribagh to be sly, cunning and a Raja with no self respect. Influenced by this fear that the European troops would cross Chutupalu Mountain road and enter Ranchi, Umrao Singh and his supporters wanted to obstruct the mountain road. The rumour regarding the European troops had been spread by Shambhunath Singh.[4]

Road Obstruction

Thakur Vishwanath Shahdev had expected that Tikait Umrao Singh would obstruct the enemies from passing the mountain road. From the military point of view, Tikait Umrao Singh was the keeper of an important mountain pass. Dalton had tried to win over Umrao Singh anyhow to his side. In his letter to Umrao Singh threat of hanging had also been given. Shambhunath Singh had prejudiced Dalton against Tikait Umrao Singh. There was pressure from all sides on Tikait Umrao Singh but he was made of different mettle.

Umrao Singh discussed the matter with his younger brother Ghasi Singh and Diwan Sheikh Bhikhari. It was decided that the route from Chutupalu to Charughati pass which was a part of the kingdom of Umrao Singh should be damaged. Taking with them some men, these 3 brave men of Ormanjhi started the work of cutting the pass. The pass had itself been quite narrow from the beginning and dangerous too. Cutting the route at certain places and digging ditches would make it very difficult for the soldiers to reach till Ormanjhi.

Umrao Singh utilised his limited strength to the full to aid Thakur Vishwanath Shahdev. He sent the message regarding his work done to Vishwanath Shahdev and the rebel soldiers. News regarding the damage done to the mountain pass reached Shambhunath Singh of Hazaribagh and thereafter to the British authorities.

It was not easy to obstruct the mountain road by cutting it at various places. Due to this work, the problems of the British increased. At that time the names of Tikait Umrao Singh, Ghasi Singh and Sheikh Bhikhari had become prominent in the list of enemies of the British. The freedom fighters had high hope on the Doranda soldiers.

The effort of the Doranda soldiers to go to Jagdishpur to meet Babu Kunwar Singh proved fatal. These freedom fighters should have taken the Palamau route, not the Chatra route, because it was safer. The British govt. wanted to keep the G. T. Road free for easy flow of traffic. Hence it would have been safer to go via Palamau which was far away from the G. T. Road. The businessmen of Chatra also did not support the freedom fighters. So, for how long would the freedom fighters have fought on an empty stomach ? Therefore, on 2 October 1857, the troops of Major English which were well armed with adequate weaponry, proved to be stronger than the freedom fighters who were either captured or scattered.

Doranda cantonment was desolate. Col. Dalton did not face any obstruction when he entered the cantonment. This signaled the return of the British govt. to Ranchi.

After stabilizing, Commissioner Col. Dalton started to catch the rebels and to hang them thereafter. In this processs, Tikait Umrao Singh, Ghasi Singh and Sheikh Bhikhari were arrested. Tikait Ghasi Singh was incarcerated in Lohardagga jail where his death took place.

Tikait Umrao Singh and his Diwan Sheikh Bhikhari were arrested. On 6January 1858 prosecution case was started against them and as expected, Tikait Umrao Singh and Sheikh Bhikhari were sentenced to death. On 8 January 1858 they were hanged from 2 branches of a banyan tree in Chutupalu.[4]

In India, British administration was based on terror and fear. The Govt. wanted to take advantage of all those occasions which would terrorise the Indians. In specific places or areas, it was announced from before that so and so rebel would be hanged to death there the next morning.

Judicial Commissioner William Oakes was supposed to be present during the hanging of Umrao Singh and Sheikh Bhikhari. There was an overwhelming crowd from nearby villages and it went on increasing. Seeing the continuously swelling crowd, Oakes had not wanted to remain there for long. Both freedom fighters were quickly hanged and leaving their bodies hanging from the branches of the banyan tree, Oakes hurried back to Ranchi.

List of Reference books

1. Bihar District Gazetteer Ranchi, Patna, 1970, Pg. 57
2. P. Kumar, "Madho Singh and the Sheikh that after them the road to Ranchi through Ormanjhi would remain closed for the enemy. " op.cit. Pg.126
3. Dalton to Young, "..... be liable to exemplary punishment" of hanging and forfeiture of his Ghatwali Estate, if it was found that the roads, ghats and streams

in question had "been purposely in jured." No. 7 at 21 Aug. 1857, Home cons No.30, dt. 18 Sept. 1857, Chhotanagpur Commissioners Des, Vol. 218.

4. Dalton to W.H. Oaks, "An attack upon the Ichak palace of the residence of Ramgarh Raja" Hazaribagh, 8 Sept. 1857, Home Cons. No.30, dt. Sept. 1857.
5. Bihar District Gazetteer Ranchi, "Tikait Umrao Singh and Sheikh Bhikhari were sentenced to death on 6th January and executed only 2 days after." Pg.61.

Chapter : Nine

Nilambar – Pitambar

(In 1857 when Jharkhand was often echoing with the war of independence of the soldiers, Palamau was involved in the tribal freedom struggle, the leaders of which were Nilambar and Pitambar).

Nilambar and Pitambar

In the process of war of independence of 1857, the most agitated district of Jharkhand was Palamau. Actually there was less of sepoy agitation and more of public move ment.[1] The Chero and Kharwar tribes are predominant in Palamau's population. These tribes are divided in various sub-seats. "Bhokta" is a predominant sub-sect of the Kharwar tribe. Brave, enthusiastic and firm in racist feeling, the Bhoktas used to live in between the high hills of Palamau and Sarguja. There are many hill roads and passes there which were in the possession of the Bhoktas and they were their source of income. In the view of the British govt. this was a looting and uncontrolled, troublesome race. The chief of this race had died while enduring the pain of exile, Nilambar and Pitambar were the 2 sons of this rebellious chief. After the death of their father, the fiefdom of this area along with a token land rent was awarded to them with the aim that being involved with the affairs of the zamindari Nilambar and Pitambar would remain quiet.

Nilambar and Pitambar mainly organized the Bhoktas but did not keep the organization limited only to Bhoktas. Not only Kharwar but also Chero tribals got themselves included in the organisation. At the time when talks were going an about the organization, Pitambar was in Ranchi and he had clearly seen how the soldiers were freely forcing the British to leave the country. On his return to Palamau he recounted how the 8th Native Infantry troops were freely moving on the roads and the British rule was over.

The sepoy mutiny of Ranchi had affected Palamau. The morale of the freedom fighters who had participated in uprooting the British rule was quite high, so much so that the fiefs and zamindars who had been loyal to the British became worried about their own safety. The organization of Nilambar and Pitambar had received good cooperation. Along with the Bhoktas the whole Kharwar tribe had been organized. In addition, getting the assurance from Nilambar and Pitambar that Chero will continue to sit on the throne of Palamau, some prominent Cheros joined the organization. In this way a strong organization that could challenge the British or British-supporters had become ready.

It had been observed that most Rajput jagirdars (fiefs) or zamindars were supporters of the British. They used to fully assist the British, and the British trusted them. One such Rajput jagirdar was Thakur Raghuwar Dayal Singh who had his fiefdom at Chainpur, about 3 Kilometer from Daltonganj on the southwest. He was number one on the list of Nilambar and Pitambar. After him were Shahpur and Leslieganj. Under the captaincy of Nilambar and Pitambar on 21 October, 1857 their organized troops attacked Raghuwar Dayal Singh but Raghuvar Dayal Singh successfully defended himself. After Chainpur, Nilambar and Pitambar attacked Shahpur. From there they could get 4 guns. Making the local thana surrender to them, they attacked Leslieganj. The police and the gunner ran for their lives.[2]

Palamau remained disturbed in the whole month of November. Lt. Graham along with 50 soldiers reached Palamau. He got the news that some Bhoktas were going towards the hills of Sarguja, but Lt. Grahman felt insecure to rush after them with such few soldiers. He went to the fort of Thakur Raghuver Daya Singh along with his troops and remained there. Assessing the number of soldiers with him at that time to be insufficient he had asked for more soldiers. He had reached Chainpur on 7 November, 1857 and from that time onward, fearing the rebels, he had more or less become arrested in the fort and had asked for more troops for his own protection. Major Coater came from Sasaram with 2 companies of force and he freed Lt. Graham from the fort.

Rajhara Station[3]

The rebels had spread in various areas of Palamau district. The British army was not being able to surround them. Apart from the Bhoktas, some rebels in small groups would plunder and loot at opportune moments. The Bhoktas mainly targeted govt., semi. Govt. or companies working with the govt. so that they they would leave the country lock, stock and barrel. Such a coal company was working at Rajhara station. Coal used to be loaded at Rajhara Station. Two officers Grundy and Melja were looking after the work of that company. There were some staff also working under them.

Very soon a huge crowed of armed Bhoktas surrounded Rajhara station and drove away the workers. Grunday and Melja had carefully placed themselves at the side and disappeared from the scene. The Bhoktas looted and plundered and damaged to their hearts' content and thereafter returned. The aim of that drive was to show that there was no govt. in the country. This incident took place on 27 November, 1857.

The increasing pressure of the soldiers

Lt. Graham, who had now been freed from the siege of the rebels, as per direction reached Shahpur where on 8 December the army had already reached. With the coming together of Graham's troops, the strength of the army increased. The Raja of Deo alongwith his 600 soldiers joined the main troops. During the organizing of the troops, an important leader of the revolutionaries Devi Baksh Rai was caught.[4] This affected the organization of the rebels and thus they got scattered. In the meantime Lt. Graham had freed the Patan hill road of the revolutionaries. There was now no. use left of the rebels who had surrounded Chainpur. Hence, they returned. During their return they attacked Ranka fort but met with no success.

The Chief of Sarguja sent a group of 600 soldiers to help Lt. Graham. As a result, the military capacity of Lt. Graham had increased to such an extent that not only was he feeling completely safe but also had acquired the strength to attack. He received information that the circle in-charge Premanand belonged to Kharwar tribe and was a confidante of Nilambar and Pitambar. Graham attacked him and defeated him.[5]

As per the next programme, the historic fort of Palamau was the target. This fort was fully utilized by the revolutionaries. Capt. Dalton himself was directing this drive. He reached Manika on 21 January 1858. Lt. Graham joined him alongwith his troops at night. It was decided that instead of wasting time, attack should be launched immediately. The rebels were hiding in the fort. Dividing the troops in 3 parts, the fort was being surrounded from 3 directions when bullets were fired from the fort but which were directionless. This firing clearly indicated that the rebels were in the fort. Bullets were fired from both sides. It seems that keeping the soldiers engaged in gunfire, it facilitated the rebels to quietly escape.

The gunfire had stopped. Upon entering the fort, 10 dead bodies were found. There was one casualty and 2 injured amongst the soldiers. Apart from rations and weapons, a knapsack was found in which letters addressed to Nilambar, Pitambar and Haklant Manjhi were found[6] and which Amar

Singh at the directions of Thakur Kunwar Singh had written. Apart from boosting their morale, sending help had also been said. The letter indicated that Nilambar-Pirambar were not only local leaders, but also recognized at Bihar level.

Attack on Chemu

Till now all efforts of Capt. Dalton remained unsuccessful. These two leaders of the Bhoktas, Nilambar and Pitambar freely worked for setting up their organisation. Dalton who was connected to the effort of collecting soldiers at Leslieganj was of the firm view that he would thoroughly comb the entire hills of Palamau and Sarguja so that the rebels would have no room for escape. Dalton collected about 2000 soldiers. He also called a meeting of all the jagirdars of Palamau.

Dalton divided his troops into 3 groups. One group was placed under "Kishun Dayal Singh and others". They were supposed to got to Baghmara mountain pass of Shahpur and handle its security. Dalton along with his troops occupied Tungri Ghati i.e. Tungri mountain pass. The rebels had fled from that place. Thereafter Dalton targeted the country of the Bhoktas. Dalton thought of adopting all the tactics which would force Nilambar and Pitambar to surrender.

Dalton, along with his troops, entered the country of the Bhoktas without facing any resistance. Chemu village, situated on the banks of the River Koel, was the village of the leaders of the Bhoktas Nilambar and Pitambar. Dalton had reached Chemu on 13 February 1858. He had resolved that anyhow he would arrest those two rebel leaders. The village was desolate. The villagers had gone and hid behind the hills. Enough food grains were found during the search of the houses. Saneya was a village close to Chemu and was a solid stronghold of the rebels but this village, too, lay desolate. There was nobody in the houses who could have been interrogated.

Dalton was not willing to return hopeless. Sometime or the other, the villagers would return to see their dilapidated houses. Thus with that thought in mind, he stayed there along with his troops till 23 February. Dalton ordered his cavalry men and the soldiers to check the hills thoroughly. The soldiers meticulously carried out the combing operation but met with no success. Camping for a long time of 10 days had been of no use. He had used all the policies of conciliatory means used in politics, the political stratagem of winning the enemy by giving gifts, giving punishment, and cause disunion through divisive politics, but without any result. There was no information about the secret hideout of Nilambar – Pitambar. Most of the people of Palamau were very much committed to their beloved leaders.[7] Although Nilambar Shahi and Pitambar Shahi could not be caught, Capt. Dalton did not think that they were still very dangerous.[8]

Although Nilambar – Pitambar had no connection with the revolutionary soldiers yet they were, as public representatives, working against the British administration in a big way. They had been connected to Kunwar Singh and Amar Singh. When Dalton had raided them, they had escaped from a secret passage but their knapsack had been recovered from a place. In the knapsack, the letters of Kunwar Singh and Amar Singh had been found. The letters had encouraged them to hold out against the British, administration from Palamau fort, so that some of the soldiers would remain engaged in Palamau. The other Kharwars and Cheros also gave support because whatever doubts the Cheros had, Nilambar – Pitambar had done away with. Hence, the Cheros who had at first maintained distance from Nilambar – Pitambar had thereafter come nearer to them. Nilambar – Pitambar were also getting support from some zamindars, and the Bhatts of Tori started waiting for further indications from them.

Dalton had nearly lost and with this comment that Nilambar Shahi and Pitambar Shahi were no longer that dangerous, expressed self-satisfaction. Suddenly he received information that both brothers were assembling in a family feast. Dalton surrounded that place from all four sides and ultimately succeeded in arresting Nilambar and Pitambar.

After a brief hearing of the charges against Nilambar and Pitambar, they were sentenced to death by hanging. They were publicly hanged from a mango tree. In achieving martyrdom for the independence of the country, Nilambar and Pitambar became immortal in the history of Jharkhand.

List of Reference Books

1. Bihar District Gazetteer Palamau quotes P. C. Roy Choudhary, "….. But the district that was most severely affected was Palamau. In this district the whole country side was aflame and it was a real national uprise…… There was less of the movement from military but more from the civil population." Patna, 1961, Pg. 70.
2. K. K. Dutta, "They attacked Chainpur….. were opposed there very strongly by its Thakur Raghubar Dayal Singh, who was devoted to the interest of the British Govt. " …… Unrest in Bihar, Patna, 1957, Pg. 77.
3. Bihar District Gazetteer Palamau, Patna, 1961, Pg. 72.
4. K. K. Dutta, op. cit. Pg. 78.
5. Bihar District Gazetteer Palamau, Pg. 72-73.
6. K. K. Dutta, op. cit. Pg. 79.

7. Bihar District Gazetteer Palamau, "...... But neither threat nor promises had any effect in inducing them to reveal the hiding places of their chief." Pg. 74.
8. Ibid.

Chapter : Ten

Telenga Khadiya

(The promoter of Jury-Panchayat, Telenga Khadiya, believed that such kind of panchayat if they spread in the tribal country's villages then the country would automatically be freed from the foreigners).

Telenga Khadiya

Amongst the martyrs of Jharkhand the contribution of Khadiya tribe in the form of Telenga Khadiya was a very important one. Telenga Khadiya was a thinking person, and in his view, apart from the British govt. the other enemies were the zamindar/ contractor and the moneylender whom he wanted to drive out from his land. For this an organization was needed. When an empowered, organized society would come up parallel to these exploiters then the solution would itself come out. There was requirement to find out an opportune occasion. Telanga Khadiya had thought about the subject very seriously and thereafter he presented his proposal of "Jury Panchayat" before the intellectual people of society. There was a speciality in him that before finding out a solution to any problem, Telanga would go to its roots.

Telanga Khadiya was born on 9 February, 1806 in an ordinary farmer's family of village Murhu, Thana Sisai, district Gumla. His father's name was Thuiya Khadiya and his mother's name was Peti Khadiya. Some people believe that Telanga Khadiya was born in 1840 but most people believe and fix his birth year as 1806. The father of Telanga was the store Keeper of Chhotanagpur's Nagvanshi Maharaja Ratugarh. He also used to look after his agriculture and cultivation.[1]

It is said that Telanga in his childhood days was an intelligent boy and his thinking power was very sharp. In order to prove himself right he would argue very well. He was very talkative. In Khadiya language a talkative person is called Tebblanga. It appears that this was the reason why he got the name of "Telanga". He had not done much of schooling but his practical knowledge was good. At the appropriate time he got married to Ratni Khadiya in 1846. By that time Telanga knew how to shoot arrows, how to use the sword, how to strike with the hatchet and how to skillfully brandish the mace. He had also started to impart education to some disciples at home. During childhood he had been going with his father to the Royal court where he had experienced the pressure of the British administration. He used to see that the zamindars and money lenders of Chhotanagpurs were ranged on the side of the British govt. and thought that in order to face them the villagers should be trained in the use of traditional weaponry.

Jury Panchayat

Telanga Khadiya had developed the idea of "Jury Panchayat" to fight the British, zamindars and moneylenders. He wanted to establish "Jury Panchayat" in every village. Jury panchayat was a youth organization of the village which used to train the villagers in the proper handling of weapons. In addition, training was also given regarding administrative structure or organisation and how to run it well-in short the importance of such knowledge for better administration. The main centre of Jury Panchayat was the "akhara" of Sisai. The villagers used to come to this "akhara" for getting training. Telanga Khadiya used to teach archery to the youths as their mentor. Fighting with swords and sticks were also taught. The number of trained soldiers in the akhara had gone up to 1500. These trained people used to go back to their villages where they established Jury Panchayat, and this is how one by one the villages developed skilled armed fighters. Accordingly, by spreading from village to village, the Jury Panchayat became a big power.

Apart from Sisai, the active branches of Jury Panchayat, where the youth took training, could be found in the following places : Murgu, Jura, Doesa, Soso, Numtoli, Dundariya, Tetauli, Madhima, Nathpur, Bendaura, Kolebira, Mahanuang and Kumhari village.

Before taking training, the people connected with the Jury Panchayat had been given the directive to hoist their flag in the eastern direction, kneel down, and remember Singbonga, Mother earth, Sarna mother, Sungod, Mahadaan god as also their own ancestors.

In the meanwhile, Telanga's father was thinking of something else. He wanted to give Telanga's future a definite direction. He used to meet the Maharaja and the other officials of the court accompanied by Telanga, and wanted that his post should be given to Telanga. There was no difficulty in this. It was customary in the Royal court that the place of the father used to be given to the son. Telanga's father Tuiya Khadiya used to reach the harvest of the Majhias villages to the storehouse of the Maharaja. He used to also look after his own cultivation. But Telanga was of a different mettle. He talked to his father about his organization and how much the "Jury Panchayat" had been extended.

Telanga Khadiya became busy in his work. He personally met the people of East, West and south Gumla and encouraged them to stand up when the time came. The name of Telanga Khadiya was on the lips of everybody in Gumla, Lohardagga and other areas. The moneylenders as well as the zamindars were terrified. Those who had come in contact with Telanga were very desirous of repeating the scenario of 1831-32. The police and daroga of the nearby thana had become anxious. The govt. had received the information about the preparation of Telanga Khadiya, and the police had received the orders to arrest him. The police were, thus, after him.

Living incognito and arrest

Telanga left his home and took refuge in the forest from where he continued to run his movement. At times he would come to the village where he would meet members of the Jury Panchayat and give them directions. Thereafter he would go back to hiding in the forest. The police had started troubling Telanga's parents because it believed that he would surely be coming to meet his relatives at home. A policeman had been stationed a little away from his home to keep constant vigilance over it. It had also happened that news had been received about Telanga's presence in a particular village but by the time the police could reach there, Telanga would have moved off some where else.

In order to keep his organization alive it was necessary to go to the villages. But it was difficult to keep safe from the zamindars and their men. Ultimately, when Telanga Khadiya was addressing the members of the Jury Panchayat of Kumhri village under Basiya thana, the police reached there and arrested him. His students and local citizens tried to block the police but Telanga asked them to maintain peace. Telanga said that the organization is greater than the individual. Individuals come and go but the organization keeps on living. He asked them to keep the Jury Panchayat organized through their combined efforts which would lead finally to victory for them.

It was hoped that the "Ulgulan" which had been started would be carried on to victory by the warriors of jury Panchayat with the cooperation of the soldiers and the public.

It was through "Ulgulan" that the lands of the tribals which had been forcibly taken away by the moneylenders would have to be returned. By giving loan at high interest rates and to keep the land mortgaged and thereafter to misappropriate them was an old business of the moneylenders, the result of which would be seen in the revolt of 1831-32. Although due to Wilkinson's rules, the procedure to misappropriate land had stopped, but the zamindar, police, govt. officials and moneylenders were cast in the same mould. They had been exploiting the tribals for years. This Ulgulan would re-establish the tribals in power. In one Khadiya folksong there is mention of Ulgulan against the police and touts in which it says how Telanga and his colleagues used to wage guerilla warfare from the forests and Jungles[1]

In this way, ulgulan increased between Telanga and the touts and police. The attacks by Telanga were like guerilla warfare. His weapons were traditional. When war took place, Telanga and his colleagues left their homes. They started living behind the fences of gardens and orchards, or cover and glens of the forest due to which he was given the name of "Rata Tetenga". When sending information in the forest, instead of Telanga, the name "Rata Tetenga," was used.[2]

Telenga Khadiya and his "Jury Panchayat" had become a terror for the zamindars and money-lenders, His next step was to implement among the money-lenders and the loanees the orders passed by the Panchayat. Telenga Khadiya's plan was to set up a parallel govt. at the tribal level which would function as per tribal tradition. But before he could give a practical form to his plan, Telanga was arrested. Although the members of the Jury Panchayat were aware of the next programme, the arrest of Telanga deeply affected the organization. After a summary hearing, in which he was charged for setting up an organization against the govt., probably instead of death by hanging, Telanga was sentenced to life imprisonment and sent to Calcutta jail.[3]

According to family sources, after going through 14 years of imprisonment, Telanga returned to his village. Due to good behaviour sentence used to be lessened in jail. He appeared to be a quiet and docile convict. Hence his punishment had been reduced. Most people say that Telanga returned after 19 years while some others say that his incarceration was for 18 years.

Some people had taken it for granted that after this long period the fire that had been burning within Telanga had been put out, but still his return to his village was not liked by the zamindars and money-lenders. They had thought that while undergoing this long imprisonment he would either die or he would quietly sit at home. Still, his return was sufficient reason to give sleepless nights to the rich and govt. officials.

After his return from Calcutta, Telenga Khadiya had kept quiet for some time. He was being rejuvenated by the soil, water and air of his village. Alongwith this, the contact with his old supporters began firing the old Telanga within him. He had wanted to see all the jury panchayats for once. If the jury panchayats were still there, then the village youth must be coming for training in the akhara, so then what grievance did the govt. have against him ? The British govt. had declared him to be guilty just because the zamindars and moneylenders had complained against him.

Telanga started moving in the old villages. Within a few days, the jury panchayats started to come to life. The general revolution of 1857 had been put down. The British and the zamindars loyal to them were in an exhilarated mood. In 1857 new arrangement regarding land rent had been started which had increased the burden of the peasants. Many revolutionaries of Jharkhand had been hanged.

Hundreds of rebel soldiers had achieved glory of warrior's death. The Christian Missionaries were prospering and under the protection of the govt. they were spreading fast. Telanga had never thought that within a few years so much of development would take place in Nagpur, especially the spread of Christianity and the increase of morale of zamindars and money leanders. Telanga got involved in his work with alacrity. New youth were inducted in the village jury panchayats and new life in the work-procedure of Sisai akhara was introduced. Every day at a fixed time Telanga would reach the akhara and after getting his disciples go through prayers, he would start their training.

The zamindars and money lenders were watching the increasing anger of Telanga. They had thought that after experiencing the torture of prison life that old man would become slack, but Telanga was spitting out more fire. Police was now quiet. The money lenders used to complain to the thana in charge that Telanga had become more violent than before but the thana in charge used to say that when an incident would take place then only the police would come into action. The money lenders and rich capitalists of the area were the most frightened of Telanga. They had been informed that Telanga used to burn the loan documents. The money-lenders asked for assistance from the zamindars. Now there was only one way left Telanga should be destroyed.

23 April, 1880

As always, Telanga reached the Sisai akhara that morning where his disciples were present from before. He had bent for prayer like always when the sound of a bullet was heard. The disciples stood up. They saw that the body of their guru Telanga Khadiya was covered in blood and writhing on the ground. Death had taken place. The disciples lifted the body of Telanga and after passing through thick forests across the Koel river to village Soso, Neem toli, Gumla, his body was buried in an upland. Even till date that upland is famously known as Shaheed "Telanga Tope Tanr (upland)."[4]

It is said that Telanga Khadiya was killed by Bodhan Singh, a professional killer. He had been hiding in a nearby bush and during the prayer he was waiting for the disciples to bend for prayer. As soon as the disciples bent, he pressed the trigger. It is said that at that time the age of Telanga Khadiya was 74 years.

The whole life of Telanga Khadiya was dedicated to his country and tribe. His plan of jury panchayat was an armed preparation to root out the British govt. and the exploiters from his land. He had been charged with sedition and imprisoned in Calcutta jail. After undergoing long imprisonment for 14 years, his revolutionary life instead of cooling down, had increased in sharpness. Just like heated gold a radiance could be seen in his face. The 14 years of jail had made Telanga more respected. The disciples of Telanga used to take pride that they were his disciples.

Telanga's murderer Bodhan Singh who was resident of Khargaon, Sisai, became heirless.[5] There is no stream available of his family. The only son of Telanga, Jogiya Khadiya, left Murg village alongwith his family, shifted to Virkera Ghagra Awas which is in Jamgai Panchayat within the jurisdiction of Sisai thana. The descendants of Jogiya Khadiya work as Pahan (Priest) in the village.

In the history of Jharkhand, there is hardly any dutiful son who had to undergo the torturous life of the 14 long years of imprisonment. The time period of his punishment proves that Telanga Khadiya had been accused of sedition. In this way, Telanga Khadiya's life as a martyr started from his jail incarceration and ended with his murder by the loyalists of the British and the exploiters of the tribals.

List of Reference Books

1. Dr. Susheela Kerketta, Veer Shahid Telanga Khadiya, Jan Hul, Hindi Masik, Ranchi, Pg. 7.

2. Ibid.
3. Ref. Telanga Khadiya, File No.: 133, dt. March 3, 1855, Lohardagga Collector's Despatch Vol. 1855.
4. Where there is Bazar Tanr now, Telanga's Akhara had been there.
5. Based on hearsay.

Chapter : Eleven

Bhagirath Manjhi : Founder of the Safahar Movement

(In Santhal Pargana, Bhagirath Manjhi gave message to the tribal society suffering from inferiority complex that their religion was excellent and superior and their society was the best).

After the revolution of 1857, 2 elements enthusiastically came up in great form in Jharkhand-one, the British administrative officer and, two, the Christian missionary. While converting the adivasis, the missionaries filled their minds with feeling of inferiority that they were semi-civilised and worshippers of ghosts and spirits.[1] Thus their lands were being forcibly taken over and they were helpless to take any action. The ideas related to the tribes were given solid publicity by the contemporary European historians, anthropologists and writers so that at the international level the British rule and the conversions being done by the missionaries could be justified. This is the reason that when the tribals took up arms to protect their land, their respect and rights, they were dubbed to be murdersrs, plunderers and trouble makers and thereafter were cruelly suppressed by the military.[2] Actually, this situation was very sad. The adivasis had nearly accepted that their religion was more or less affected by ghosts and spirits and that they were born to serve the others. In this situation, several learned groups of society and social reformers encouraged their tribes to live with dignity and self-respect. They had explained to their people that their religion was excellent and superior and their society was the best. This country had been handed down to them by their ancestors. Due to this, several reform movements took place, the Safahar movement was one of them.

Safahar or Kharwar agitation began in 1871. Its originator was Bhagirath Manjhi, inhabitant of Taldiha.[3] He said that the main reason for the pitiable condition of santhals was to forget their ancient religion. If the Santhals wanted to improve their condition then they would have to bring back the religion of their ancestors and establish it again. Famous as Babaji, Bhagirath Manjhi was directly connected to Chando Bonga (Santhal God). The Santhals believed that whatever Babaji desired, he would get it done by Chando Bonga.

Babaji stressed a lot on cleanliness in his sermons. Safahar in the combination of two words-Safa+har. "Safa" means clean and fresh, and "har" means acceptance. The message was that everybody must stay clean and fresh. Babaji wanted to put an end to the custom of rearing poultry and pigs. He emphasized on regular bathing and having faith in God. According to him not only is it necessary to stay clean but it is also essential to have cleanliness of our inner character. Discussing the sacrifice of Siddhu-Kanhu, babaji told his followers that these 2 brothers had won Santhal Pargana and the Santhals would have had their rights over the country but during the revolt the Santhals became characterless. They started having physical relations with women of other races[4] due to which God became angry with the Santhals resulting in their defeat. Hence, Babaji stressed on inner and outer cleanliness. The Santhals accordingly destroyed their poultry and pigs, but instead of throwing away their carcasses they thought it better to eat them for the last time. That is how, from then onwards, one group of disciples of Bhagirath came to be called kharwar.[5]

In the meantime, in 1874, Santhal Pargana faced famine. The Santhals began to face starvation deaths. Everywhere there was a hue and cry to save the people from starvation. The British officers were experiencing difficulty in maintaining law and order. To lessen the effects of famine, rice was imported from Burma[6] and distribution was arranged from the manjhi sthan (akhra) of the Santhals. Bhagirath Babaji told his followers that the rice offered by the Santhals to God Chando Bonga was being collected by the "sahibs" on the direction of Bonga for distributing it to the Santhals. In this way, the rice offered by the Santhals to the bongas was being returned.

After some time, the govt. staff were sent to the area of the Santhals to collect the dues of the rice distributed among them where, however, they faced a lot of difficulty. Actually the message spread by Babaji became the reason for the difficulty being faced in collecting the dues. When this information reached the higher Officers, they issued the order to arrest Babaji. The police arrested him and in front of everybody, sent him to jail. When the Santhalis came to know the reality, then some of them started to despise Babaji, while some others considered it to be atrocity of the British.

Bhagirath was charged with inciting the people against the govt. and to indulge in rioting through them.

After his arrest, Bhagirath Manjhi receded to the background, but the safahar movement initiated by him continued. The number of Babaji's followers swelled like flood. Some scholars dubbed it as "good business to earn money." This truth cannot be denied that whoever flaunted himself as a "baba" (holy man) in those days his intention was to earn money, but Babaji while earning money, gave the following main directions to his followers.[7]

(1) Every creature has been given by God so do not kill any creature.

(2) Maintain purity in food habits, behaviour and living.

(3) Do not use hurtful language.

(4) Do not hit animals otherwise God will punish you. Protect the grazing grounds of animals so that they can easily graze.

(5) Sunday is the day of rest. You yourself rest on that day and let others rest, too.

Babaji needed money for living, for arranging for his workers, and for other works. The need for money is an admitted truth but money is not everything. Babaji used to awaken respectful feeling in the minds of followers towards people, society and religion, and this was the main aim. He joined the safahar movement and carried out his responsibility within his area of work. Safahar movement was running this way in small constituents.

Getting Godly basis and support, Babaji used to cure the ailments of the faithful followers who came to him for relief. In some of his directions, Babaji used to give the advice to not pay land rent to the govt. because the land had been the property of their ancestors. But most Babajis used to limit themselves to religion and society, avoiding politics to be out of trouble. If any Babaji dabbled in political area, then coming within the attention of the administration, he too would be sent to jail just like Bhagirath manjhi. This had become a good source of income and good business[8] which they did not want to destroy.

In 1880, Duwiya Gosai, resident of Jagesah took over the leadership of the Kharwar Movement.[9] In this movement, he gave written and verbal instructions to the Santhals about religious reform. The written order was sent to far off places saying that whosoever would disobey the orders of Gosai he would be punished by God. In this, such examples had been cited which surely affected the people. He instructed that as per previous order, there should not be poultry and pigs at home or in the neighborhood-everything must be clean. Gosai also proclaimed that whatever he does, he is actually implementing the orders of God. Verbally, as well as through letters, publicity was made that by the next Vijaya Dashami they would have their own rule during which rent free grazing ground, if buffaloes ploughed the fields then one rupee and if bullocks ploughed the fields then eight annas rent rate would be payable. An economy that would be developed would be without money-lenders.[10]

The Kharwar movement got fresh energy under his leadership. The movement had reached Ranchi after passing through Giridih Govindpur. Although in Ranchi area, this movement could not be very effective, still people started waiting for that day when the British would be driven off from the country and Babaji's rule would be established. The festival of Vijaya Dashmi came and went. The British and Babaji remained as before. When people criticized Babaji, then Babaji became agitated and explained that on Vijay Dashmi night God told Babaji that they were fallen people. When the Santhals would deserve their own rule, then automatically they would get their own Raj. A nearly similar proclamation had been made by the Kharwars in 1881. Now the Kharwars had started believing that they were superior to the other Santhals. The Kharwars had tried to intimidate the other Santhals through their organized power and strength. Due to this, Col. Thomas Gordon had to be in readiness as the head of District military police and 4500 field force in Dumka,[11] though, no untoward incident took place.

Safahar movement was a reformist movement. The Santhals knew that the period or age of their ancestors was golden age. In matters of religion, society, wealth and property, they were at the top. The Kharwars tried that the Santhals should place their religious and social life in front of the golden age of their ancestors and cleanse them accordingly. Ghosts spirits, bonga which had entered Santhal life, they would have to be driven off. Similarly there were many evil customs which had deeply entrenched themselves in their religion and society. The Santhal religion and society would have to be cleaned of them.

The Babaji types of people played an effective role in making the safahar movement meaningful. The Babaji people were spread in the four directions of Santhal Pargana. Every Babaji had his own sphere of influence. This area, spread over 8-10 miles, had the Babaji as its centre. In this area, the Santhals followed their religious and social life according to the Babaji. Although all the Babaji advised the same social and religious behavior, get there were some in whom local elements gave them a separate identity.

In the later part of the safahar movement, it was marked that the movement veered towards Hindu religion and Hindu way of life.[12] The influence of Hindu festivals and celebrations was clearly reflected on the Santhals. Some Kharwars who used to call themselves safahar, joined in having faith on Mahadev. The Santhals living in the neighbourhood of Hindus or coming in contact with them were influenced by their wealth and prosperity, and their living style. The thinking and living style of the Santhals were affected by the contact with Hindus. Some Santhals who used to call themselves Safahar could be found worshipping Mahadev regularly. It may be mentioned that some Babajis had started being worshipped by their followers as if they were equal to gods.

With the passage of time it started looking as if the movement was finished. But it had not ended-it went underground which during times of scarcity and famine kept revealing itself. In the famine of 1919 it had its role to play though a small one.[13] With the passage of time this got divided in 3 groups-Sapai, Samra, and Babaji.[14] Despite many attacks-counter attacks and rise and fall this movement started in 1871 as Safahar movement gave a new direction to the thoughts and life style or acceptance or way of living to the Santhals.

List of Reference books

1. S. C. Roy, "Munda and their Country," quotes Report of German Mission "Let us grive up demon worship, become Christians" Pg. 153.
2. J. C. Jha, "And when the people rose in protest they were treated as marauders or rebel, and hunted down by the troops," The Tribal revolt of Chhotanagpur, Kashi Pd. Jayswal Research institute, Patna, 1987, Pg. 47.
3. L. S. S. O. Malley, "Bengal District Gazetteer Santhal Pargana," Logos press, second Indian Reprint, Delhi, 1999, Pg. : 146.
4. Ibid, Pg. 146.
5. Ibid, "After this the people commenced to kill their pigs and Fowls ; but they were wise enough to eat them. From this time the followers of Bhagirath Manjhi appear to have taken the name of Kharwar," Pg. : 146-147.
6. P. C. Roy Choudhary, "Bihar District Gazetteer Santhal Pargana," Secretatiat Press, Bihar, Patna, 1965, Pg. 952.
7. L. S. S. O. Malley, Pg. : 147.
8. L. S. S. O. Malley, Lucrative Profession Pg. : 149.
9. L. S. S. O. Malley, Pg. : 147.
10. V. Veerotham : Jharkhand : History and Culture : Bihar Hindi Granth Academy, Patna, 2006, Pg. : 331.
11. P. C. Roy Chowdhary, "Bihar District Gazetteer Santhal Pargana," Secretariat press Bihar, Patna, 1965, Pg. : 952.

12. L. S. S. O., Malley, Pg. : 149
13. P. C. Roy Chowdhary, opp. Cit. Pg. : 953
14. Ibid, Pg.: 180

Chapter : Twelve

Birsa Munda

(About a century ago from today, the dream of "Munda Raj" seen by Birsa and shown by him to the citizens of the country, that came true on 15 November 2000 with the coming up of "Jharkhand Raj").

Birsa Munda

The most celebrated and proclaimed name among the martyrs of Jharkhand is that of Birsa Munda. It is such a popular name that from a small school to the university, from a small shop in a lane to big institutions of the Govt. they are well-known by this name. A time comes when a person gradually fades away and his ideals and aims cast their shadow-over the people and his name keeps his identity in the form of a symbol. A martyr is a martyr. His greatness has its own place but behind the martyrdom of Birsa Munda the ideal of Birsa Dharam (religion) and Birsa Raj were alive. The follower of Birsa, with a white flag, continuously fought the British rule for his rights. This is the reason why the name of Birsa became the symbol for a movement. Such is the background of the prestige and immortality of Birsa.

There is a controversy among the historians about the birth place of Birsa Munda. Some learned people think it to be Ulihatu, some say his birth place is Nawan, others alongwith proof believe Kundi village to be the birth place of Birsa Munda. According to this group, there are many folk songs pertaining to Birsa Munda prevalent in Khatanga village. In these songs lively mention has been made of Birsa taking birth and practising archery with his bow and arrows on Khatanga buru. Khatanga buru is the northern extension of Kundri. It is clear that the birth place of Birsa Munda is Kundi.[1] S. C. Roy has said that Birsa was an inhabitant of Chalkad.[2] The Mission school, Chaibasa, in which |Birsa had studied for a few years, records Bamba as his birthplace.[3]

Birsa's father's name was Sugna Munda. He was distressed with poverty and so he used to go from village to village looking for work. Troubled with extreme poverty, Sugna accepted Christianity and his Christian name was Masih Das while Birsa was named "Daud." Birsa's father, on recognizing the intelligence of his son, got him admitted to Mission school, Chaibasa for proper education. Birsa remained in the school for three years. Within this time he saw the frandulent claims of the missionaries and their opposition by the sardars. One day Father Nortrat while teaching the students said that "if you become Christians then your land will be restored to you," but this promise was never fulfilled. Birsa had criticized the Father for giving false assurance due to which he was thrown out of the school. Birsa had started despising the Fathers and the Christian religion. Birsa returned to the faith of his ancestors.[4] Birsa had remained in Chaibasa from 1880 to 1890.

The period of evolution

A glimpse of the revolutionary nature of Birsa was seen when he criticized the advice of the Father before his class mates. Birsa thought it unjust to endure wrong words. At that time his intellectual hunger was increasing day by day. In 1891 he came in contact with Anand Paur. Anand Paur was not a pundit or a learned scholar. He was Swansi by caste whose main profession was to weave cloth. Anand paur was working as a clerk with Jagmohan Singh, zamindar of Bandhgaon. He was a Vaishnav by faith. He had good elementary knowledge of the Ramayana, Mahabharata and the Puranas. By being in contact with him, Birsa could see a clear direction that right at first a person should maintain purity of behavior. He should be far away from meat, fish, and liquor, he should have daily bath, he should worship, apply a stroke of sandalwood paste on his forhead and put on the sacred thread. Whoever believed in Birsa religion should have a tulsi (basil) altar out home.

Birsa had learnt from Anand Paur some incantations to cure maladies and had also acquired knowledge of some medicinal herbs. Over a time period, this knowledge proved very useful. Birsa was a very intelligent young man, and used to take full benefit of situation. Now he had developed as a good looking, handsome youth. His well-formed body, pleasant face and speaking style were very attractive. Apart from this, some incidents happened which helped in making Birsa worshipful as God.

This incident is of June 1895 when Birsa was crossing the forest alongwith a friend. The sky was overcast. Suddenly there was very bright lightning. Birsa's friend noticed that Birsa's face had acquired a red lustre and an ethereal glow was upon him.[5] Birsa was still on the forest path when his friend reached the village and narrated about the ethereal glow of Birsa. When Birsa returned, he found the villagers waiting for him.

There were many incidents connected to Birsa about healing the sick. He used to wear wooden slippers. He used to wear dhotis of 3 different colours-turmeric coloured dhoti in the day, white dhoti thereafter, and blue dhoti at night. Birsa's name and religion had spread in distant places. When people used to come to meet him, they would bring rations for another day with them. Father Hoffman of Sarvada Church has written about the people who used to come to Birsa to meet him- "The distance of my mission centre (Sarvada) was at a distance of only 9 miles from Chalked. The centre used to see daily the innumerable people coming in lines from different parts of the country to that village. These people either came to hear his preachings or to get themselves treated. In some cases of treatment there was failure but the people were not discouraged because they thought that Dharti Aba (Father Earth) was the reason which meant that there was no dearth in the capability of Birsa to cure diseases but since the unsuccessful patients lacked faith and confidence in Birsa, they could not be cared."[6]

Birsa was a person of extraordinary intellect. He used to wear wooden slippers. His dhoti used to be yellow due to colouring by turmeric. The sacred thread used to adorn well his strong physique. There used to be an ethereal glow on his face. Whenever somebody came to him for treatment, Birsa used to read some incantation and blow upon the patient. He used to caress the head of the patient with his hand. Sometimes he used to give some medicinal herbs to the patient. Birsa's fame had reached Singhbhum. Birsa was at first known as "Rog - har" but later on he became preacher of Birsa religion in the form of angel of God. The fame he had gathered at first as Rog-har came in good stead to support the establishment of Birsa religion and its publicity. The main aim of the crowd which used to reach Chalkad from far off places was to have a glimpse of Birsa and to listen to his sermons. As time passed, the followers of Birsa spread information of such incidents among the Birsa faithful that Birsa came to be believed as an angel of God. The preachings and sermons of Birsa started getting a lot of importance. In Birsa religion, purity in conduct and food was considered compulsory. Wearing of the sacred thread and worshipping the tulsi plant was a necessary part of Birsa religion. The faithful followers of Birsa had docile, simple and nonviolent life-style. The number of followers of Birsa kept on increasing gradually.

The entry of Sardars

The coming together of sardars in the Birsa movement is a mentionable incident. During those days, one of the root problems being faced by the tribes of "Chhotanagpur was the return of their lands from forcible occupation. The missionaries took great advantage of this problem. They had converted many tribals to Christianity by giving them the assurance that they would pressuries the Govt. and get their lands restored to them. Despite a long wait, there were no results whatsoever.

Well known as "Sardar," these people were converted tribal Christians, and they believed that if the Fathers of the mission pressurized the govt. then the lands could be restored but these Fathers would do no such thing. Hence the sardars opted for legal process. In this context a quarrel took place between the sardars and their mission, resulting in the sardars thinking to set up a new mission. Some people thought that those sardars were fraudulent and dishonest.[7] There sardars used to collect heavy donations from their own areas in the name of fighting these cases in Calcutta High Court. This was also another form of income for the sardars. They knew that they would lose the cases but still they collected this money. As has already been mentioned, the Sardars were not fallen. One sardar Godian was a teacher in Lutheran School. Another Sardar Prabhu Dayal was assistant to Birsa.

According to Father Hoffmann, these sardars went from village to village, giving wide publicity to the divine power of Birsa that, he could cure incurable diseases. According to Father Hoffman, the crowds which used to come from various villages to Birsa was the result of the publicity given by the sardars. Hoffman in his letter written to Forbes had mentioned the influence of the sardars due to which the Birsa movement started taking a political turn.[8]

The sardars were converted Christians. They used to accuse the Fathers of their Christian religion that while converting them the Fathers make big promises but later on they forget them. These sardars rebelled against the mission and used to fight legal battles against the govt. that the system of "baith-begari, rukmats, enhancement of rents of Rajhas land" etc. should be stopped forthwith.[9] According to the sardars, it was the responsibility of the missin to restore to the tribals their rights, but the mission was not coming forward for it. Hence the sardars had to come to the forefront. One weak point of the sardar was that they had collected donations to fight the legal cases but they had kept no account of the same.

Birsa had seen in Chaibasa that when the govt. had by law declared the forests as protected, then the sardars had started an agitation for the restoration of the traditional right to use the forests. Hence, Birsa's opinion of the sardars was good. After losing the case, since there was no other programme, the sardars had started scattering. Looking at the vast public support of Birsa, the sardars started to join the Birsa movement. Father Hoffman commented thus on the sardars- "A drowning man will catch a straw."[10] Actually the sardars had no other programme. The sardars wanted followers and crowds, and Birsa had both. The influence of the sardars could be glimpsed in the thoughts and speeches of Birsa.

Birsa was seen as a religious preacher. He had proclaimed himself as a prophet. The govt. was anxious but not active till then. The very fact that crowds in thousands were coming to meet one person could have created administrative problem at any time. This was the reason why the area zamindar, thanedar (Police station in charge) or people of the mission were all the time feeling afraid and pleading with the govt. of giving them protection. But the legal fight put up by the sardars against land related injustice had deeply influenced his (Birsa's) thinking. In his preachings, while starting with religious matters he would very soon switch over to the atrocities being committed by the zamindars.

Birsa declared in one assembly that in that year no sowing would be done. As a result, the agricultural fields remained dry. A local govt. officer was angry at this madness of Birsa. Although some rumour regarding group killing had been spread that the foreigners would be exterminated, Father Hoffmann remained undisturbed by this information and spent the whole night in Sarvada church. Birsa, in a crowded assembly, also proclaimed that the rule of Queen Victoria had ended and the Munda rule had started.[11] He also declared that now the lands were rent-free.[12]

Arrest

Till 22 August 1895, no action was taken against Birsa. The Commissioner did not want to give any importance to him. In his view, Birsa was probably a mad man. He was apprehensive that Birsa might cause breach of peace. In this context, the Deputy Superintendent of police G. R. K. Mayers was to serve arrest warrant under sections 353 and 505 of the Criminal Procedure code of India. The penal provisions of the sections related to obstructing govt. employees from carrying out their official responsibilities, attacking them or using criminal force.

In the context of section 353, Lakshman Lal, head constable of Tamar, who had gone to Chalkad with some sepoys to arrest Birsa, had submitted a report which is illustrative. Birsa had been staying in Chalkad in a hut from 9 to 16 August. The report is full of contradictions. But, it is true that the head constable of Tamar Thana had gone to arrest Birsa but was unsuccessful.[13] In this way, Birsa and a few persons were guilty under section 353.

Section 505 relates to such statement, rumor or giving report, publishing it or giving publicity due to which there would be apprehension of breach of peace.

The Deputy Superintendent of police had been instructed to arrest Birsa in a peaceful atmosphere. No weapons should be used. The strength of Birsa lay in crowds, hence he should avoid crowds. With full precaution, Birsa was arrested while sleeping. This was on 24 August.

The news of Birsa's arrest spread quickly from village to village. There was apprehension that the crowd of followers would suddenly attack and free Birsa, but nothing of the sort happened. When the whole party reached Ranchi, then it was four in the evening. He was brought before the Deputy Commissioner. The court room was filled to capacity. Normally among the sensible people there was an understanding that Birsa was crazy and had an unbalanced brain. There was serious discussion regarding this matter.

The falling of the wall

That day it was raining heavily yet the crowd of visitors did not decrease. By the time the court proceeding ended, it was seven in the evening. The paperwork to send Birsa to jail had already been completed. The sepoys took Birsa to jail. It was just a coincidence that as soon as Birsa entered the jail, a thick mud wall crumbled and fell. The faithful of Birsa had exaggerated this incident in their discussions and had expressed their belief in the divine powers of Birsa.

From the time when the Tamar police had come to arrest Birsa and returned disappointed, Birsa had feared that the British govt. would soon arrest him. When there was talk of arrest, then the crazy god within him came out with the statement that he would be in jail for maximum three days after which he would be released.

From far-off places Birsa's faithful followers started coming to Chalkad. On the third day, Chalkad was overflowing with these followers. Approximately 7000 people had gathered in Chalkad.[14] They were fully hopeful that their god would appear in Chalkad after three days. But this did not happen. On the fourth day, heart broken, the crowd started to return.

Peaceful, discouraged, with bent heads the crowd was returning. Their path went past the front of the Sarvada Church. Father Hoffmann tried to talk to them but they did not even glance at him. Birsa's forecast of being released from jail was proved wrong but also his proclamation of "agni varsha" (rain of fire) was proved a lie. They were themselves feeling defeated.

The Deputy Commissioner and other high officials decided that the very fact that the Mundas had started believing Birsa to be God was the root cause of the problem. Hence to show that Birsa was also an ordinary person, his case was transferred to Khunti. Mundas are in majority in Khunti. When Birsa will behave like an ordinary person in front of the Mundas then his appearance as a savior will be brought crashing down to reality. But the situation that developed was totally opposite to what those officers thought. Mundas started crowding in front of the jail. They started putting pressure to have a view of Birsa, and brought about an uproar. It appears that the sardars used to join these Mundas. The regular coming together of Mundas in this manner outside the jail created an additional problem for the administration.

The Deputy Commissioner while passing order on the case of Birsa, discussed the connection of the sardar with the faithful followers of Birsa due to which the followers of Birsa became very violent. Birsa was accused of generating hatred against the British govt., of causing loss of revenue, and propagating the ineffectiveness of ammunition. It was also written in the order that Birsa had told the people not to pay any rent. He had also propagated the end of the Queen's rule and the beginning of Birsa rule.

In the background of the aforementioned accusations, Birsa was sentenced to two years of rigorous imprisonment with fifty rupees fine. In lieu of fine, six months of additional jail term would be applicable. The followers of Birsa were also punished. Although the officials and zamindars heaved a sigh of relief after sending Birsa to jail, Munda Raj or the seed of freedom which had been planted among the people was difficult to be done away with. It was one matter to catch Birsa and put him in jail, but the more difficult task was the planting of the seed of Munda Raj in the population on which no officer's attention had been drawn. Without proper nurturing, the seed could have withered away. But this did not happen. Birsa was not physically present in Chalkad but his teachings were deeply penetrated in the very breath of his followers.

Rebellious Birsa

On the occasion of diamond jubilee celebration of the rule of Queen Victoria, amnesty had been granted for the convicts of the empire. Birsa also benefited from this and before he could complete his prison term, he was released from jail.[15] During his jail term, although outwardly Birsa was quiet yet within he was burning, thinking how he would complete his unfinished task.

After coming out from jail, Birsa tried to show his rights in his paternal places. On the basis of gotra (clan) and totem it is proved that the ancestors of Birsa while crossing the river had used a billet of wood. In that log there had also been a rat. Admitting its obligation, the ancestors of Birsa themselves adopted the Chutupurity kili. Since Birsa was of Purti Kili, hence Chutia was thought by him to be his ancestral place.[16] Birsa alongwith some of his disciples threw away the idols installed in the Chutia Mandir (temple), broke them up and fled. Arrest warrant was again issued to arrest Birsa.

Birsa believed that the copper plate denoting right of his ancestors to the Chutia area must have been kept in the Chutia Mandir. His aim was not to break the idols but to search the copper plate which may have been kept beneath the idols. He was unsuccessful in finding any copper plate. Seeing the activities of Birsa's disciples, some people along with the watchman gathered there upon which Birsa's men ran away. They stood accused of breaking and damaging the temple and arrest warrants were also issued, but actually Birsa's real aim was contained within his disciples only.

Under these circumstances, Birsa thought it more useful to work underground. He went to Jagannath Temple to take food offered to the deity and to obtain blessing, and also went to Navratangarh, Doesa to bring sacred water "Veer-da." Imprisonment had changed the direction of Birsa's thinking. Birsa abandoned Chalkad to make Dombari his work place. In Chalkad, Birsa's appearance as a prophet had been developed but it was in Dombari that he came out as a "freedom fighter." The natural surroundings of Dombari are favourable for freedom fighters. This place was protected on all four directions by high hills. There is only one route leading out which opens in the hill route of Domba. Another specialty is that there is an open space for people to assemble and there is provision of water.

During his incarceration, Birsa compared the strength of the British govt. and the strength of the Munda tribe and found that if there is a confrontation some Mundas would die, some Mundas would undergo rigorous imprisonment, and their children would starve. Hence it would be proper to abandon the path of violence and adopt the path of non-violent righteousness and accordingly try to set up Munda Raj.

The first secret meeting took place in February 1898 among the Mundas who had come from far-off places in Dombari at the residence of Jagari Munda. Birsa placed his side before all the Mundas and said that before any step is taken the overall fall-out should be carefully considered. Hence Birsa said that they should discuss the matter with the other Mundas about how to get Munda Raj (rule)- whether they should adopt the path of violence or the path of righteousness and non-violence.

Some Mundas expressed their opinion that the route of law and power has many hurdles. The British are very crooked and mischievous and so long as they are not beaten and thrown out, the Munda country cannot be made independent. This was a difficulty question therefore it was postponed for the next meeting.

The next secret meeting took place on the Simbua hill on the day of Holi, March 1898. The Sarvada church could be seen from there. Nearly about 200 followers of Birsa had participated in that meeting. They were in agreement with the principle of Birsa. Munda explained to the congregation that there was no dearth of resources with the British. War of righteousness would give them victory otherwise they would have to face rigorous imprisonment and their children would die of starvation.

The meeting continued till late night. In this congregation the sardar-supported Mundas had also participated. They were bent upon violence. Marmi, Jharu Munda and Prabhunath Munda had been given the responsibility by Birsa to go to the Munda areas and explain to the Mundas that the path of violence would be the reason for the destruction of the Mundas, but if they adopted the righteous path then in future Munda rule could be established again. The sardars who used to economically exploit the Mundas were not in agreement with Birsa. Birsa was sad.

Police came to know about the congregation at Simbua the next morning. Plantain leaves and other litter scattered at the place made the police easily calculate about the late nightassembly. The area police was assured that Birsa Munda would appear after dark, at night. That is why the police became inactive and quiet.

Uncertain Birsa

After spending some time in prison, Birsa acknowledged that nothing would be gained through path of violence. He used to reason with the Mundas that 2-3 years of punishment would mean that they would undergo rigorous imprisonment while their wives and children would go through unbearable hunger. What would they get ? Therefore, to re-establish Munda Rule the path of righteousness and non-violence was the best.

The young leader of about 22-23 years while speaking to the congregration would become violent. He used to ask his followers to keep their weapons ready. In February 1898an important convention took place in Dombari. In this convention, Birsa had explained the justification of the path of non-violence but in the end the voice of revolt had erupted from his throat.

There were other secret meetings and Birsa gradually became violent. Now he began telling his followers to gather weapons. This movement was to be started on 24 December night meaning from the start of the festival of "bada din" (Christmas). During the case, the description of the arrangement of the convention was as follows :

"We reached the meeting place slightly earlier then midnight. The meeting was taking place on the top of the hill. When we reached, about 60-70 people had already assembled there. Birsa was sitting on a stone on which a sheet had been spread. He was sitting facing the east. The rest of the people were sitting all around. By midnight most of the people who were supposed to attend had reached the place. The moon had come out and the meeting started in the moonlight. Birsa asked the congregation as to what were the problems they were all facing. Some people, whose names I do not know, got up and said that they were deeply troubled by the exploitation and suppression of the zamindars, jagirdars and contractors. Thereupon Birsa said that we should learn how to make bows and arrows and hatchets because we are very much tormented. Birsa also said that in other meetings he has ordered to make weapons. Birsa further said that with these weapons they would kill the contractors, jagirdars, kings, officers and Christians."[17]

Although in every convention Birsa used to talk about preparing weapons but he was uncertain about the form of the movement and its success. He knew that the Europeans could be frightened by arrows and arson. Birsa believed and had faith in public might. He wanted that the Mundas in the name of organized strength should be called back from Christianity and absorbed in the Munda organization. At first our ancestors came and cleared the land and set up Munda country. There after, a king was set up and to meet his expenses donations were obtained and given to him. Later on this donation, took on the form of land rent.

If all the Mundas come together for the sake of Munda raj, then the white skinned would leave Munda country which would result in the re - establishment of Munda Raj, but Birsa could not do anything as per his plan. The influence of the new sardars in his organization was increasing. There was not much time. On 24 December night, the Sarvada Church was set on fire and arrows were shot at the Fathers aimlessly.

Birsa was undergoing tough mental tension. He wanted to include the Christian Mundas in the name of Munda Raj in his movement. He believed that in the name of ancestral heritage and Munda brotherhood, they could be made to agree that every Munda would, on the ground that their field and lands were gifted to them by their ancestors, unite in stopping payment of rent. This would affect the British govt, this would be a kind of quiet movement which was a symbol of organised strength of the Munda. But Birsa could not do this. From the proclaimed night of 24 December, arson and rain of arrows began.

Father Hoffmann used to stay near Chalkad and understood pretty well the high flying thoughts of Birsa. In his letter written to Deputy Commissioner Forbes he has said that based on his past experiences he had started thinking that the Govt. had wrongly interpreted the true aims.[18] Thus, if he could attract the vast public towards himself them the govt. would not take any serious step against him. The Birsa followers thought that if their Christian brothers joined them, then their movement would fully acquire the nature of being a Munda racial drive.[19]

The area of the rebels was widespread. In addition to Singhbhum's Chakradharpur, Ranchi's Khunti, Karra, Torpa, and Tamar and Basiya's church and Padres were on target. One nayak had small organized troops each consisting of 8-10 followers. Their aim was to set the Churches on fire and to drive out the fair-skinned padres from the country. According to Father Hoffmann the godown of his Sarvada Church was set on fire and when he came out with the last Father an arrow was shot at him. Nearly all the arrows missed their targets. Birsa had special anger against Father Hoffmann. The Father had special knowledge of Munda language and was also dear to some Mundas. Birsa Munda was of the opinion that since Father Hoffmann knew the Munda language well, through spying he could easily gather information which he would pass on to the British govt. hence, one arrow was targeted at Father Hommann which hit him on the chest but it being the cold of December, Father Hoffmann had been wearing an overcoat over several layes of clothing. As a result the arrow could not pierce all those clothes to touch his body.[20]

The Porahat sector of Singhbhum was very much affected by arson. The German Mission church of Kundugut was set on fire. A German trader was killed in Sonpur area. The revolutionaries were working in a controlled manner. The incidents of arson were much more but there was no news of anybody killed. Till that time of the revolt, another mentionable detail was that the zamindars, moneylenders or outsiders (dikkus) had been deliberately protected.

News about the revolutionaries had been reaching everywhere. Seeing the extensive area of the revolution, the Deputy Commissioner of Ranchi had estimated that the number of the rebels was large and that they were fully disciplined. In order to surround the rebels and to catch Birsa, an area of 150 aquare miles of Singhbhum district were identified as also the following :

(1) 300 sq. Miles area of Khunti and Tamar.

(2) 100 sq. miles of Ranchi district.

With the identification of these areas, police pickets for regular protection were posted in them. The expenditure had to be borne by the local population.

Bandhgaon is situated in the middle of Ranchi-Singhbhum road. The zamindar of Bandhgaon, Jagmohan Singh, used to be afraid of Birsa and his men although as a youth Birsa had spent 3 years as a student of Anand Paur who had been the munshi or clerk of the zamindar Jagmohan Singh. In this way Birsa was fully acquainted with Jagmohan Singh. Although Jagmohan Singh used to be afraid of Birsa because he acknowledged that he himself was responsible for the crimes committed by him, but Birsa easily let him go.

The control room of the identified areas of Ranchi and Singhbhum, where the police were working, was set up in Bandhgaon. This was for the ease of police activities. The administrative officers believed that Birsa would be caught in that area. Search for followers of Birsa could also be carried out there. The calculation of the police officers was not wrong. Secret meetings used to be held but Birsa would not be present there. His message used to be delivered in those meetings.

The difficulties of Birsa

Consequent to the Chutia Temple incident, warrant of arrest against Birsa had been issued. To evade arrest, he had to go underground. Hence he could not participate in the secret meetings. He used to frequently change his places of stay. Gradually, the grip of Birsa over the organization grew slack. The sub-leaders took their own decisions regarding the incidents to be carried out. The crowd had increased a lot. The entries of the sardars had become whimsical. Birsa wanted to reach out to the public with his ideas and thoughts so that they would come over to his side but the way Birsa wanted to do it, his followers were unable to do it with finesse. Due to this the opposite was the result. That Birsa who wanted to become popular among the people through his thoughts and deeds, he was now being termed as equivalent to a terrorist.

Based on his past experience, Birsa's strategy had undergone a sea-change. Now he talked about his closeness with the zamindars, money-lenders and other dikkus (outsiders). There were only two enemies-one, the fair skinned padres. He told them that they should return to their own country. And, two, the fair skinned British sahebs. Birsa said that it is better to have less number of enemies so that it would be 140 easy to fight them. If all the tribals and all the Hindus came together on one platform, then their victory was assured. Birsa's thinking was a far-reaching one. If all the Nagpuris came on a common platform, then the padre and the sahel would run away to Europe.

The first phase of Birsa's movement was against the padres. On 24 December night, attacks were conducted in their own sector on the Churches.[21] But the zamindars and others did not know that they were not the targets of the movement, but were actually protected. This should have been propagated among the public but this did not happen. Hence, the zamindars, moneylender and others were terrified as before. Birsa's thoughts remained with Birsa only.

The second phase of his movement which started in January 1900 was against the white sahebs, their houses, office and thanas. The movement started properly. Some people joined on the way with weapons as a result of which the very form of the movement changed although the main aim had been to get public opinion in his favour. All these twists took place because of the entry of the new sardars.

From 25 December 1899 to 5 January 1900, the situation was peaceful. Actually it was quiet on the surface but preparations were going on within. Father Pushing of Burju church had mentioned to Father Hoffmanne about the hard labour of the Mundas going on in the forest and the activity of the followers of Birsa, and similar information was conveyed by the Father in his letter in which he wrote- "Now the Munda people are assembling in the jungles and apparently their intention is to come together and go in for a collective revolt and to give stiff opposition to the police and army."

The next meeting took place in Juiri. In that meeting anxiety was expressed that the followers were not working as per written aims of the organization. They should find out such a way that the ordinary people do not become terrorized by themrather they should welcome them. How to implement these aims in a practical manner was to be discussed in the next meeting which would take place at the residence of Gaya Munda.

After Birsa Munda went underground, the next name which came out prominently in the organization was that of Gaya Munda. Gaya Munda was creating anxiety in the minds of the police-administration and missionaries. The Deputy Commissioner Streetfield thought it necessary to arrest Gaya Munda. Birsa Munda's going into hiding was proving harmful for his organization. Most of the time he had made the thick forests of Singhbhum his place of shelter. The residence and main work area was Atikedi.

Deputy Commissioner Street field who had been putting up in Bandhgaon had gathered information about Gaya Munda from before. He left for Atekedih alongwith the daroga Iltaf Hussain and some sepoys and reached at about 11.00 a.m. when they surrounded Gaya Munda's house. This incident took place on 6 January, 1900.

The daroga Iltaf Hussain asked them in Mundari to come outside. Within the house about 8-10 people were found comprising of adults and children. The daroga again called out twice in Mundari that they should come out, but there was no reaction from within. The Deputy Commissioner showed his pistol and fired a shot in the air. Ultimately the Deputy Commissioner took a match stick and set fire to the hut. The hut started blazing. All of them came out brandishing weapons. Gaya Munda was brandishing a sword. This went on for some time. Suddenly the Deputy Commissioner jumped on Gaya Munda and fell on the ground along with him. Gaya Munda was below and Streetfield was on top of him. The Deputy Commissioner said that he had held fast to his wrist.

Since Munda was down and the Deputy Commissioner was on top of him, Gaya Munda's wife was beating him with a stick. The Deputy Commissioner in his report informed that the resultant hurt could not have any effect on him. The flames of the fire were spreading and now they had come close to that place where Gaya Munda and the Deputy Commissioner were grappling with each other. The sepoys lifted them up and manacled Gaya Munda. All of them were arrested.[22] Below, in the valley, about 200 Mundas were standing with weapons in their hands.

The firing at Sayil Rakab

The hill of Sayil Rakab is at a slight distance from Dombari and about three miles north of Saiko. Right from the morning of 9 January 1900 the followers of Birsa had started reaching the hill. Slowly, the Mundas who were to take part in the meeting had reached the place. It is believed that in Khunti these were the very rebels who had attacked. Police had already got the information that the rebels were going to hold their meeting in Sayil Rakab. The Deputy Commissioner joined the police force to carry out the decision of surrounding Sayil Rakab and to attack it.

When the police alongwith their officers reached the foothill of Sayil Rakab, it was 11 a.m. Commissioner Forbes decided to climb up a nearby hill top. Between this hill and Sayil Rakab was a deep ravine but both hills in one place were connected by a hill route. When they crossed Tirilkutiburu and the preceding ups and downs and reached the hill top it was one O'clock in the afternoon.

The officers called out in Mundari in raised voices to the Sayil Rakab Mundas, giving then warning that they should put down their weapons and surrender otherwise they would be shot. Efforts were made to make them understand but the Mundas had more confidence in their weapons and more faith in Birsa's words which were "the guns will become wood and bullets would become water" but still there were many other Mundas who had started searching for places that would hide them and protect them.

The police party went on foot to such a place on the hill from where talks could be held with the rebels. Commissioner Forbes, through the help of translators, tried to make the Mundas understand and warned them that if they did not listen, they would be fired upon. By now, the police and army had reached near the rebels so much so that the rebel Mundas had comewithin the range of police bullets.

As a warning, one round was fired. Nobody was injured, which proved that the forecast of Birsa that bullets would turn into water was correct. In the second round of firing some people were seen falling on the ground. The Mundas shot arrows and used slings but to no effect. Now it was necessary to act. In the meantime, some Mundas were going down the hill and disappearing in the forest. Hence, Commissioner Forbes instructed Deputy Commissioner Streetfield to go down with some sepoys so that the fleeing Mundas could be arrested.

Thereafter Forbes directed the police and the troops to move forward and commence firing from the hill top. This was the third round of firing.

This had a direct effect on the rebels. Encouraged by this, Forbes ordered them to move further onward and fire. It was fruitful for the Deputy Commissioner to go to the foothill along with his sepoys because the rebel Munda sepoys who had come down from the hill to run away were caught. Meaning which, the meeting could not take place and some Munda men and women were shot down.

Commissioner Forbes had given clear cut instructions to his reserve police and army officers to take recourse to minimum firing and for self-defense. But this did not happen. The reserve police and the army had one after the other reached the hill-top and fired from there which proved mortal. The rebels had either run away or taken shelter in the hill caves or else got killed by the gunshots. Probably despite the instructions of the Commissioner, bullets were fired. Even the fleeing rebels were made targets of the bullets. In the process, corpses of three women were also recovered. Firing upon fleeing rebels was an inhuman villainy. Some Mundas had run away with their dead. Authentic figures of the number of dead women and men could not be available but it was definite that compared to govt. figures the number of the dead was much more. Some of the dead bodies were quietly buried in a nearby ditch dug up for the purpose.[23]

It is a hard question that when Birsa's faithful followers were facing mortal danger during the firing in Sayil Rakab, where was Birsa ? Birsa normally never participated in the daytime meetings. Some of Birsa's disciples had pleaded with him to stop at Bortodih which Birsa had accepted. A woman called "Sali" was kept there to look after him. Birsa went away from Bortodih to the house of his maternal grandfather at Apuvhatu. After residing there for a few days when the sddiers started reaching there also, Birsa disguised himself and went off to Marangdaha. News was received that from there he had gone to Singhbhum.

In the aftermath of the firing incident of Sayil Rakab, some very debatable matters came to light regarding the number of the dead. The govt. had published a list containing the names of the dead and their number, but it was not believable. Lt. Governor's office had criticized Commissioner Forbes regarding the "firing incident," especially "the firing of bullets on the fleeing women".

The Mundas had felt the effect of the Sayil Rakab firing incident and the local administration thought that the Birsa movement would breakup and scatter. It was true to a certain extent, but Father J. B. Hoffmann, who was known to be very knowledgeable about the Mundas, wrote in his letter to Commissioner Forbes that the followers of Birsa should be dealt with very strictly because they were very stubborn and a tribe which did not easily change.

According to Father Hoffemann, to live under the illusion that due to this incident there has been any slackening in the firm resolve of Birsa's men would be a big blunder. The Father advised the Commissioner to take as much strict action as possible against Birsa's followers. He also advised that the movable properties of his followers should be attached or confiscated. His further advice was to stop all channels of reaching food and rations to them, to arrest some of the leaders and boys, acting as roving spies, and put them in jail till Birsa got arrested, to prevent the wives of the leaders to leave their villages and to go anywhere else. Father Bayer had also advised that the gram pradhans (village headmen) and mankis of the villages falling within the zone of influence of Birsa, should submit a guarantee paper or agreement paper that in their villages no activity pertaining to Birsa Munda would happen and anybody related to such activity will not be allowed access or stay in that village.[24] Community arrests would also help in crushing their morale.

Commissioner Forbes had termed the advice of Father Hoffmann as full of boastfulness. To arrest an innocent Munda on the basis of mere suspicion was not justice. The Commissioner clarified that Govt.'s aim was not to launch a religious war against Birsa's religion but to suppress with strictness any effort to disrupt peace. People who had played active role in the revolt, should not be compelled to go underground and participate in open revolt. Such a situation would have arisen as a reaction to Father Hoffmann's advise of community arrest.[25] Rev. Father John Baptist Hoffmann not only among the Roman Catholic Mission but also among the Fathers of all the missions was the most Knowledgeable about the Mundas.[26] Influencing proficient and British administrators for manipulating the work process as per his convenience was his expertise. Encouraged by his own proficiency, Father had written a letter of advice to contemporary Commissioner Forbes. The tone of the Father's letter made it appear to be unnaturally prejudiced. There was a lack of objective and impartial thinking. Father Hoffmann had failed to see Birsa as a religious mentor in whom ideal thoughts of conduct and behavior were inherent.

Birsa dharma (religion) gave out message of abstaining from meat and wine, and to follow the path of truthfulness and fidelity. What shortcoming was there in Birsa religion which was based on non-violence? But it was a challenge to Father, and his action denoted his hopelessness. As to sedition and attacking govt., buildings or terrorizing, these were being tackled by the Commissioner, Deputy Commissioner and officers of the army who were active and facing these problems. To control such situations, they had more knowledge and experience than the Father. Under the circumstances, it was clear that the letter written to the Commissioner and especially in his suggestions the defeated anger of Father Hoffman was speaking. This is the reason that the Commissioner commenting upon the advice of Father Hoffmann had turned it as "full of boastfulness". The suggestion of Father for community arrests had also been termed as unjust.

Birsa had great influence in that area and no Munda was ready to adopt Christianity. But in the absence of Birsa, there used to be increase in conversion to Christianity. Govt. officials used to commit atrocities on the people following Birsa religion. The Mundas who wore the sacred thread were asked about the address of Birsa and if they were unable to give the answer, they would be beaten up. The Christian Mundas escaped such atrocities. It has been seen that govt. employees gave more facilities to Christian Mundas compared to ordinary Mundas. With the break-up of the Birsa movement, it was found that the crowd of Mundas increased in the churches.

The stern steps taken by the administration consequent to the Sayil Rakab firing incident, namely, arrests, confiscation of moveable property, etc. gave satisfactory result. Normally the Mundas had broken down, and some wellknown Mundas were surrendering in front of the officers. Most of the people had started thinking that the Birsa movement was nearly finished, but some experienced people were advising not to remain under this illusion. According to them, they were the weak followers of Birsa who broke down, but the stubborn and conservative followers were still at their jobs. It was true that the conservative followers were having secret meetings in which they were framing their future programmes. Marmi, Doka, Majhiya etc. who were the pillars of the organization were still at large and were busy with the work of the organization. The Christian Mundas, missionaries and some govt. staff were terrified by the apprehension of a big movement. But on 28 January, 1900 an unforeseen incident happened. Doka and Maniya Munda alongwith followers of Birsa surrendered before the authorities. Being very much troubled by the confiscation proceedings, they ultimately surrendered. The Govt. felt assured and the specially posted troops were recalled. Despite all this, there was one shortcoming due to which the administration was still ill at ease and that was the arrest of Birsa. But they did not have to wait for long for this.

In the ultimate phase of his movement Birsa was passing his days incognits in the hills and forests of Porhat. He still believed and hoped that with good conduct and civilized behavior the public could be attracted. In Rogoto, in a hurriedly called meeting of his followers, Birsa dwelt at length, on the Code of conduct of his followers. This was the last meeting of Birsa.

A proclamation had been made that the person who would get Birsa arrested could be rewarded with a sum of five hundred rupees. Seven people of Jarikel began planning to catch Birsa. They saw smoke coming out of the forest a little distance away. This was the jungle to the west of Santro, hence there certainly was someone. All the seven quietly crawled the distance and came near. They saw Birsa sitting there, a woman was cooking food and another woman was sitting. Birsa had two naked swords. The seven people waited patiently. When Birsa and the women were in deep sleep, all the seven suddenly caught hold of Birsa. This is how, Birsa was arrested. The incident happened on 3 February 1900.

The Deputy Commissioner Singhbhum informed the Commissioner about the arrest of Birsa. He was ordered to send Birsa to Ranchi. This news spread quickly and the crowds came on the road to have a look at Birsa. In Khunti there was a huge crowd of onlookers. Birsa had tied a turban on his head and had covered himself with a thick shawl, and was smiling at the people.[27] By giving this description the Commissioner wanted to show that Birsa had no anger against his arrest. He had taken it very normally. Similarly, amongst the collected crowd there could not be found any agitation.

Death of Birsa

On 20 May 1900 the food which was served to him early in the morning at 5:15 was returned by Birsa saying that he had no desire to eat it, but in the court lockup he admitted that he was ill. After returning to the jail, the Asst. Doctor gave him medicine. The Medical Superintendent took him under his medical care from 1 June and it may be mentioned that signs of recovery could be seen in Birsa's condition. But on 8 June his condition started deteriorating and on 9 June at 8.00 a.m. Birsa passed away. Attention is drawn to the fact that from 1 June Birsa had started recovering but on 7-8 June some such thing happened that the next morning at 9.00 a.m. he was dead. The Medical Superintendent wrote in his report that Birsa died due to cholera. He also wrote that Birsa had been suffering from dysentery from before hence he could not survive the additional disease of cholera.

People were not satisfied with the report of the Medical Superintendent. In the entire jail Birsa was the only prisoner of affected by cholera which is a contagious disease and Birsa alone was suffering from cholera. In the visceral examination, blood clots were found in Birsa's stomach and intestine. The report had also informed about the destruction of the intestines. In this way, the circumstances of Birsa's death lie shrouded till date, although according to govt. file, Birsa died due to cholera. This was a natural death and the file was closed.

Even if it is believed that Birsa was poisoned on 7-8 June, then how could such a clever person as Birsa be bluffed by anybody ? Birsa had no personal enmity with any one. From the viewpoint of his organization, he was a die-hard enemy of the Christian missionaries. Internally, the sardars wanted to deviate Birsa from his main intention so that they could establish their own supremacy. Some Mundas have taken the name of Shukdev, resident of Marcha Karora, who had mixed poison in the bread which he offered to Birsa to eat.[28] The contemporary Hindi fortnightly "Ghar Bandhu" had also expressed some what the same opinion. As per this magazine, only 2 persons were suffering from cholera, one of whom was Birsa. Birsa died earlier. Everybody used to take similar meals, used to drink the same water. The sardars could have had a hand behind this episode. It may also be that in the court, he may have been given poisoned tobacco or poisoned food to eat.[29]

Although the needle of suspicion points towards the sardars but it is a matter of the mind accepting it. A century has passed. Many scholars have worked on Birsa, done research. Books and letters have been published but the circumstances of Birsa's death have till date not been revealed. If Birsa's death took place due to cholera then several question come up. During those times, cholera was a frightful, contagious disease which used to spread fast so much so that many villages used to be vacated. In such a condition, during the time of Birsa's death in how many places had cholera spread, how many persons died in jail due to cholera, what steps were taken to wipe out the infectious bacteria of cholera in the jail etc. the answers to these questions have not been mentioned anywhere. A seminar of historians of Jharkhand should be called to decide finally whether Birsa's death was natural or due to poisoning.

The highly intelligent boy Birsa's about three years were spent in Mission Dutch Primary School, Chaibasa. There Birsa saw that the padres used to say in their preaching that if they remained Christian then one day they would get back their lands, but they termed the sardars agitating for return of their lands as knavish and betrayers. It was clear that the Church people (Christians) would never get their lands returned to the Mundas. This snare had been spread to convert to Christianity. Birsa had bitterly criticized amongst his classmates the preaching of Father Natrot. As a result, Birsa was thrown out of the Mission School. Talk of Christian religion and resurrection of prophets had been planted in Birsa's mind.

The second phase of the building up of Birsa's personality happened when he became disciple of Anand Paur. Birsa started living his life according to Vaishnav religion and accordingly adopted its life-style. The stories of the Puranas had been successful in instigating Birsa to become hero or leader Birsa learnt from Anand Paur some mantras or incantations and medicines to cure disease. The knowledge and life style learnt from Anand Paur were the basic fulcrum of Birsa's fame.

Birsa, through mantra and medicines respectively used to bring his patients back to normal health. If any patient could not be cured then it did not mean that there was any shortcoming in Birsa's mantra or medicines but that the patient and his relations were having less faith in Birsa. According to Father Hoffmann, the crowd of Birsa's visitors used to continuously pass by the Sarvada Church. Talk about reviving a dead patient had spread in all the villages.

The public crowd had made Birsa a prophet. Consequently Birsa religion started spreading. There started an unprecedented increase. in the numeric strength of Birsa's followers. The sardars, defeated from all sides, required a common platform so they joined the Birsa movement. Later on when the cases of the sardars and Birsa disciples were running, Birsa told his men that the entry of the sardars in his organization proved ruinous. The spread of his religion was enough to drive out the padres and British from the country.

Birsa's movement had clearly run in 2 phases. The first phase was concerned with religion. The target of Birsa was that in Munda country no European, Christian padre should remain. There were 2 ways for this-all the converted Mundas accept Birsa religion or come back to Sarna religion. One day earlier to Christmas, that is on 24 December evening, Birsa's disciples set fire to most of the churches in the area and rained arrows on them but no Father was frightened by this attack. It may be kept in mind that consequent to this movement, no padre was killed. Birsa had given such instructions that the padres should be tortured but no body should be killed.

The govt. did not want to describe Birsa's revolt as sedition, but to suppress the followers of Birsa the army was called out and the firing incident of Sayil Rakab had become a part of history. In order to catch the rebels or to make them surrender all possible means were tried. In the whole incident no European was killed.

At one time, in an assembly, Birsa asked his disciples as to what was their problem. The reply was the exploitation by the zamindar, moneylender. To which Birsa had said that for this the time had not come. Birsa had clearly said that if the number of enemies was increased then the movement would become uncontrollable. At that time their target was the Christian European padres and the European govt. officers. He advised them not to create another target at that time. Although Birsa was not satisfied with the zamindars and moneylenders, still they were considered as smaller enemies. Birsa Munda had wanted to run the country with the help of all the people living in the country, but first of all the country would have to be freed from the fair skinned ones. People could not understand the intention/aim behind this policy.

Birsa died in the morning of 9 June 1900. After the visceral examination, the dead body was returned to the jail. Since there were no claimants, as per jail rules, the body was handed over to the scavengers. The body was cremated in a fire of cowdung cakes near the Ranchi distillery on the banks of the river.[30] Before death and after death the widely honoured Birsa's unwept death speaks of the tale of Birsa's life of sacrifice.

The imagination of the Birsa movement for free Munda rule was absorbed in the veins of the countrymen in the form of rejuvenating blood and was transferred from generation to generation. The rise of Jharkhand State is the natural achievement of the Birsa movement. This was the reason that Jharkhand State came into being on 15 November, the birthday of Birsa Munda.

List of Reference Books

1. Purushottam Kumar, Ranchi Express (daily) dated 4 January, 1998, Pg. : 10
2. S. C. Roy, "The Mundas and their Country," Ranchi, 1995 (Reprint) Pg.: 204
3. Entry no.178, Confirmation Register, G.E.L.Mission Chaibasa.
4. S. C. Roy, "From German Protestantism, the boy soon reverted to the old Munda faith of his ancestors," Munda, Pg. : 204.
5. Ibid. Just at that moment, Birsa's companion happened to turn his eyes towards him, and was struck with astonishment at seeing Birsa's face changed for the moment from its ordinary brown-black colour to a glowing red and white, Pg.: 204.
6. J. B. Hoffmann, Encyclopedia Mundarica, Pg.: 567-68.
7. S. C. Roy, "The Settlement Officer Ranchi observed "The sardars-an unscrupulous and dishonest band of cheats." Munda, Pg. : 179.

8. Hoffmann to Commissioner Forbes, 14 Jan. 1900. Pages no.336 August 1900, Home Dep. Extract Birsa Pg.: 234 no. : 19
9. R. G. "The main grievances underlying the Sardari agitation were the system of Beth Begari, rukmats, enhancement of rents of Rajhas land." Pg. : 66.
10. Hoffmann to Forbes, 14 January, 1900.
11. R. G. ...... "the Raj of the Maharani (Queen Victoria)" was over and that the Munda Raj had commenced," Pg.: 70.
12. Ibid, Pg.: 70.
13. Deposition of Lakshman Lal, 11 Sept. 1895, Appeal no.148 of 1901 High Court Records, Patna. See also R. G. Pg. : 70
14. Dr. Kumar Suresh Singh, Birsa Munda aur unka Andolan, New Delhi, 1979, Pg. : 69.
15. S. C. Roy, "..... On the occasion of the celebration of the Diamond Jubilee of the reign of Empress Victoria, Birsa Munda was released from jail sometime before the expiry of the term of his sentence," Mundas, Pg. : 208.
16. Ibid., "A third patriarch Chuttu of Chutia Haven, the head of the Chuttu Purthi Kili, established the village Chutia." Appendix-I, Pg.: VI.
17. Deposition of P. w.- I, Ratan Munda of Kuda Emperor us Dukha Pahan and others. The Bengali, July 21, 1900.
18. Hoffmann to Forbes dt. 14 January 1900 Progs. 336 August 1900 Home Department
19. Ibid.
20. P. Ponet : A Brief Biography of Father Hoffmanne, Catholic Press, Ranchi, Pg. : 9.
21. V. Raghavaiah, Tribal Revolt, Andhra Rashtra Adimjati Sevak Sangh, Nellore, 1971, Pg. : 133.
22. Streetfield to Commissioner, 7 Jan. 1900, Progs. No.355, Aug. 1900 Home Department, National Archives, New Delhi.
23. Kumar Suresh Singh, Birsa Munda aur unka Andolan Pg.: 126.
24. Father Hoffmann to Forbes, 14 Jan. 1900, op. cit. uddhrit Birsa, Pg.: 234, no.19.
25. Commissioner to Chief Secretary 5403. Camp Heradih, 17 Jan. 1900 Progs 336 Aug. 1900 Home Conf. Public, Govt. of India, National Archives, New-Delhi, Uddhrit Birsa, Pg.: 235 no.35.
26. Rev. Fr. J. B Hoffmann, Encyclopaedia Mundarica.
27. Commissioner to Chief Secretary, no.167 R 30 March 1900 Progs. No. : 307 Aug. 1900, Home, National Archives, New Delhi Uddhrit Birsa Pg.: 235, Sankhya 39.
28. Kumar Suresh Singh, Purwodh, Pg.: 145.
29. Ghar Bandhu, Hindi fortnightly, 15 June 1900.
30. Kumar Suresh Singh, Birsa Munda aur unka andolan, New Delhi, 1979, Pg.: 144 se uddhrit.

Chapter : Thirteen

Gaya Munda

(Gaya Munda has a special place amongst the martyrs of Jharkhand because he is the first martyr with whom the Deputy Commissioner, who had come to arrest him, had to physically wrestle and whose whole family went through punishment right from hanging to even one day's rigorous imprisonment) .

Gaya Munda

Gaya Munda of sardar roots became a unique disciple of Birsa within a short time. The blood in his veins longed to drive out the foreigners and was full of patriotism to establish Munda Raj in the Country. Not only Gaya Munda but also his wife Maki was very much determined to drive out the British from Munda country. Not only they, Gaya Munda's son, daughter, and daughter-in-law were willing to confront the British. Gaya was a skilful swordsman and his son was an expert archer. Nearly all kinds of weapons used by the tribals were found in Gaya Munda's house.

Meeting in Aetkedih

Gaya Munda was a resident of Aetkedih. Before meeting took place at Aetkedih, meeting had taken place in Jiuri. The Govt. officers had now taken up the Birsa movement quite seriously. In the meeting at Jiuri, the changing strategy of the British was discussed and accordingly their own strategy was formulated and fixed. The agitationists decided to hold the next meeting at the residence of Gaya Munda in Aetkedih. This meeting was fixed for 5 January. Father Pushing, padre of Burju mission situated on the border of the area of the movement, said in his report:-

"Now the Munda people are gathering in the Jungles and it appears that their intention is to come together and revolt collectively and to face the police and the army with full force and determination."[1]

The padres were habituated to give inflated reports about the strength and might of the Mundas. Pushing had given this information to Father Hoffmann who in turn had likewise informed the Commissioner. It was true that with Birsa going underground, the Mundas had started to frequent the jungles more and more. But there was no news about preparing for any movement.

Again, Birsa had told only a few supporters about the roads to reach him because everybody could not be trusted. Hence in the secret meetings, one such meeting was called in the residence of Gaya Munda on 5 January. 5 January meaning on 4 January after 12 midnight. The Birsa followers knew the meaning of 5 January but knowledge of this meaning was not known to the police and administration.

On 4 January, the Chief constable of Khunti had to go on an enquiry to Saiko. Saiko falls in southern Aetkedih hence in this context Gaya Munda's home could have been raided. Gaya Munda was always hovering in the minds of the police and British officers. They knew that with the arrest of Gaya Munda, the Birsa Munda movement would nearly become lifeless. Gaya Munda had a good influence on the organization. The Birsa followers used to obey the instructions of Gaya Munda. Aetkedih was within the thana area of Khunti, and Khunti thana had received the information about the secret meeting called at the home of Gaya Munda.

2 constables and 3 chowkidars reached Aetkedih in the morning and found total quietude every where. They were troubled to know whether the meeting took place or not, and if the meeting took place, then when ? They did not know that after 12 midnight of 4 January, 5 January starts. The secret meeting took place right after midnight and continued till 4 a.m. About 40-60 rebels participated in the meeting.[2] Detailed discussion took place over the future preparations of the movement. Discussion also took place about the circumstances of confronting thc police. In the meeting the thought was working to a certain limit that "the gun would become wood, and the bullet water." It was thought necessary to seek instruction from Birsa on this issue.

Morning was about to appear and the eastern sky had started to glow red. The meeting was ended and the participants picked up their weapons and went away towards the east. When they reached the river Tajna, the rebels got down to the river, washed their faces and hands and sitting on the resinous parts enjoyed the fresh breeze. Some of the rebels had dispersed in the jungle maybe to go somewhere. They had received the information that some policemen from Khunti thana would be reaching Aetkedih to arrest Gaya Munda and this happened, too. Two policemen from Khunti thana, and chowkidar had found out that Gaya Munda alongwith his men had gone to Tajna river. The police party went to wards the Tajna river.

Death of a policeman

The Khunti Thana had sent 2 constables alongwith 3 chowkidars to Aetkedih with a certain purpose. In a Munda village where within a moment hundreds of armed youth would assemble, of what use would a small police party be ? Where on all four directions rebels are spread out, there a small police party can never go in forstraight confrontation and this police party met with the foreseen end.

Gaya Munda spotted the police party. He told his men that the prey had come. When the police saw the number of rebels, it understood that they would not be controlled or overpowered; hence it would be wise to run away and save themselves. One police and one chowkidar crossed the dry river and ran away towards the east, and so saved themselves. One policeman and 2 chowkidars ran towards the jungle but in the meantime Gaya Munda's son Sanrey shot an arrow which hit constable Jairam. Injured Jairam fell in a paddy field. The chowkidars fled and could save themselves. Gaya Munda along with some of his men reached the injured Jairam and killed him with hatchet blow to his head.

The chowkidars and police who had managed to excape, somehow reached the thana and described the incident in detail to the thana in charge. The thana in charge was faced with the problem of recovering Jairam's body. In the afternoon the Chief constable reached the place of occurrence and showing courage with great cunning recovered the body of Jairam and had it sent to Ranchi via Saiko. The armed group of hundreds of Mundas quietly observed the procedure of picking up the body from afar.

Challenge

The killing of a policeman by the rebels was a very big incident. The police is the basic unit of maintaining law and order. If such incidents increased then the morale of the police would break and thereafter administration would be paralysed. The Deputy Commissioner Streetfield, who at that time had been camping in Bandgaon, had been stunned at hearing this news. He concluded that this incident was a challenge for the administration. The morale of the rebels had been boosted by this incident and Gaya Munda was in the procedure to be established as the new leader of the Munda rebels.

The death of the policeman took place in the morning of 5 January. News about this must have reached the Deputy Commissioner by the afternoon. If Gaya Munda was not arrested without delay, then a wrong message would go to the Police workers. Hence, the Deputy Commissioner called the daroga Iltaf Hussain and the next day i.e. 6 January morning, prepared a plan to apprehend Gaya Munda. The next day i.e. 6 January morning, the Deputy Commissioner, daroga and some sepoys started from Bandgaon for Aetkedih.

When the Deputy Commissioner reached Gaya Munda's house alongwith his party, it was 11 a.m. Most of the members of the family were inside the house. The police surrounded the house from all sides. Daroga Iltaf Hussain was standing near the outer wall. The verandah of the house was absolutely empty. Cooked rice had been taken down from the stove and kept on the floor. Apparently the family had got together to take a meal otherwise the whole family would not have been found together.

The members of the family had sensed that the police had surrounded them, hence they had armed themselves with their weapons. But everybody was quiet. They were all informed in Mundari that they had been surrounded on all sides and it was not possible to escape. So they were asked to surrender along with their weapons because it would be for their own good. But this warning had no effect on the Mundas. Street field informed that he was their Deputy Commissioner and was ordering them to surrender. Gaya Munda shouted back that the house was his, and no body had the authority to enter his house. Despite being surrounded by the police, Gaya Munda and his family members were were undisturbed and were ready to face them with courage.

The Deputy Commissioner wanted to arrest Gaya Munda without any blood shed. He had given instruction to daroga. Iltaf Hussain that only for self defence arms should be used. But it was not as easy to arrest Gaya Munda as had been thought by the Deputy Commissioner. Gaya Munda was a Munda of very firm resolve and could never hang his head before the British.

Hatchet attack on the daroga

Daroga Iltaf Hussain along with Streetfield was trying to persuade Gaya Munda when a hatchet came through the air and hit the daroga on the head. The daroga stumbled some what but then controlled himself. Due to the turban tied on the head of the daroga, the blow of the hatchet could be endured. If the turban had not been there then the blow from the hatchet could have been fatal. In his letter written to the Commissioner from Bangaon, the Deputy Commissioner had mentioned this incident. He had also praised the daroga in it.[3]

According to Streetfield in order to frighten the Mundas, he had taken out his pistol and fired a shot aimed at the roof hoping that due to fear of the pistol they would come out but this did not happen. Munda and his family kept sitting as before. It seemed as if without bloodshed the Mundas would not come out. The Deputy Commissioner fired a shot at the arm of Gaya Munda, the intention being that the shot would result in the sword to fall out of his hand and thereafter Gaya Munda could be caught with ease. But the target was missed and Gaya Munda remained as dangerous as before. The Deputy Commissioner was not being able to take a decision as to how Gaya Munda and his family could be brought out from his house. If police resorted to bayonet charge, then there was a possibility of the bayonets being snatched. In that circumstance it would have been difficult for the police to save their own lives.

Burning down the house of Gaya

Not having any other alternative, the Deputy Commissioner decided to set fire to the house of Gaya. He gave a last and final warning to Gaya Munda to come out of the house otherwise his house would be set on fire. The screams of the Munda family asking for help and the effort of the police to catch Gaya Munda had reached the Mundas of the village and some armed Mundas could have proved to be fatal for the police party. Hence instead of giving more time it would have been appropriate to quickly arrest Gaya Munda.[4]

Gaya Munda had been shown a match stick when the final warning to burn down his house had been given. Still, when they did not come out, the house was set on fire. Due to a strong breeze, it did not take much time for the fire to spread. Gaya Munda came out with his family. Every body had some weapon or the other in his hand. His wife Maki had a long stick in her hand, younger son had a hatchet. Grandson Ramu had bow and 2 arrows. Out of the 2 daughters-in-law, one had a "dowli" and the other had a small axe or "tangi". Three daughters Thigo, Nami and Lemba had stick, sword and tangi respectively.[5] Gaya Munda was brandishing his sword. Everybody was trying that nobody should come near them.

Wrestling with Deputy Commissioner

Amongst the martyrs of Jharkhand, Gaya Munda occupies a special place. His physical fight and wrestling with the Deputy Commissioner

Streetfield is such an incident which was abnormal. When Gaya Munda and his family came out of their burning house, their effort was that police should not reach them. Hence whatever weapons they had, they were protecting themselves with those. Gaya Munda was brandishing his sword. The Deputy Commissioner's first target was Gaya Munda. With his arrest the rest would surrender. Fully considering the matter, the Deputy Commissioner aimed at the right shoulder and arm of Gaya Munda and fired two shots from his pistol. According to the Deputy Commissioner, one bullet had hit him on the right shoulder. He stumbled for some time thereafter again started brandishing his sword.

Deputy Commissioner Streetfield was astonished, being unable to fathom of what raw material Gaya Munda was made of. Even after being injured by a bullet, Gaya Munda kept on brandishing his sword as if he was in good health. Time was passing. The crowd of Mundas standing afar was swelling. The Deputy Commissioner thought that if Gaya Munda was not quickly arrested then the Munda crowd might turn dangerous, hence he shot the last bullet from his pistol at Gaya Munda. In his letter the Deputy Commissioner has admitted that he had shot the last bullet to kill Gaya Munda, but the bullet missed him.

After the pistol became empty, there remained no other resource. Hence, the Deputy Commissioner let go of his pistol and suddenly attacked him physically. Being entangled, both fell on the ground, and fighting with each other, both reached the corner of the front verandah of the house. In this entanglement, Streetfield quickly caught a wrist of Gaya. The police were silently watching this wrestling between the two. The wife of Gaya, Maki, was hitting the back of the Deputy Commissioner repeatedly with her stick. While they were thus wrestling, the flames of the fire were nearly upon them. Within a short time they would have been surrounded by the fire, hence the policemen made the entangled two to get up and brought them outside the verandah.[6] As soon as they came out, Gaya Munda and his family members were arrested. Streetfield has also mentioned about the daughters-in-law who had a baby in the left hand and were brandishing hatchet with the right hand. Gaya Munda and all the family members present were arrested.

This incident was on indication of the intense hatred the rebels had against the foreign govt. and their resolve not to bow down before it, otherwise Gaya Munda and his family would have immediately surrendered before the police party. One side of the Birsa movement was to instill immense hatred in the minds of the tribals against the British. Gaya Munda, his family, other Mundas of his village and those of nearby villages hard intense hatred for the British. Gaya was their leader. The incident of 6 January was very humiliating for the Deputy Commissioner Streetfield because the Munda daughters-in law were attacking with axes and at the same time having children in their arms. The duel between Gaya Munda and Streetfield is now a part of history but it revealed, as proof, Gaya Munda's for midable courage and bravery.

Case and punishment

Due to the numerous arrests related to the Birsa movement, there was a multitude of cases in the Sessions Court. To facilitate quick disposal, an Additional Sessions judge was posted. Due to number of prisoners being much more than the official capacity of the jail, mismanagement had spread there. There was a lot of activity in the kutcherry. Hearing of cases had become slow so much so that it would take months together for a hearing. Gaya Munda was accused of killing constable Jairam in Aetkidih. Gaya's sons were also accused for the same crime and cases were filed. Gaya's wife, daughter and daughters-in-law also faced cases based on the incident of 6 January when Deputy Commissioner Streetfield had gone to Aitkedih to arrest Gaya Munda.

Gaya Munda was hanged. He became a martyr for the sake of the independence of the country. Gaya Munda's son Sanrey who had shot constable Jairam with an arrow, had also been sentenced for hanging but his appeal for mercy to the Nizamat Sarkar was rejected and returned following which he was hanged on 22 October, 1901 at 6 a.m. Gaya's another son Jaimari was sentenced to life long exile from the country.

On 6 January, 1900 when Deputy Commissioner Streetfield had gone to Aitkedih to arrest Gaya Munda, then Gaya's wife Maki had also opposed and his daughter and daughters-in-law had obstructed his arrest. Hence for this offence, Maki was sentenced to 2 years of rigorous imprisonment. Gaya's daughter and daughtersin- law, since they had already remained in jail during the pendency of their case, were, on the basis of compassion, given the punishment of one days' rigorous imprisonment. In this way the whole family of Gaya Munda was punished. The punishment included hanging, life long exile to one day's rigorous imprisonment.

Gaya Munda was the right hand man of Birsa. Although he was of sardar Munda stock, his whole family were devotees of Birsa Munda. At the time when Birsa had not completely developed, Gaya Munda was connected to the Sardars and was busy in getting the lands of the Mundas returned to them from the clutches of outsiders. At that time the Christian missionaries were taking advantage of this weakness of the Mundas that if they would accept Christian religion and would continue as Christians, then they would speak to the govt. and get their lands returned. This was a very big enticement and the Oraons and Mundas of the village with this hope that they would get back their lands, the Mundas went on converting to Christianity. The converted Mundas at first had pressurized their own sardars, but when the promise of the missions was revealed as lies, then the converted Mundas began calling the Christian fathers "frauds" and taking the help of the lawyer Jacob took recourse to legal process.

Gaya Munda had himself faced this problem and was supporting the contractors to fight legally and try to get back the lands. Gaya Munda had not fallen into the trap of enticement by the Christians when he was very much opposed to them. Just like Birsa, he wanted to terrorise the Christians anddrive them out of Munda country. Sardar Mundas had by and large mostly become devotees of Birsa. The sardars had obtained great strength in the form of followers of Birsa religion. Gaya Munda was the chief among the Birsa devotees.

Gaya Munda has a special place among the martyrs of Jharkhand. He is the first martyr who physically wrestled with the Deputy Commissioner at the time of his arrest, and the whole family of whom was punished by hanging to even one day's rigorous imprisonment.

List of Reference Books

1. Hoffmann to Forbes, 14 Jan. 1900, Prog. No. 33, 6 August 1900, Home Department, National Archives, New Delhi, extract Birsa Munda aur unka Andolan, Pg.: 232, Kram. 8.
2. Kumar Suresh, Purwokt, Pg.: 112.
3. Streetfield to Commissioner, Bandgaon Comp. 7 Jan. 1900, Prog. No.335, August 1900, Home Department, National Archives, New Delhi, Extract Kumar Suresh Singh, Birsa Munda aur unka Andolan, Pg.: 234, Kha, No.32.
4. V. Raghavaiah, Tribal Revolts, Andhra Rashtra Adimjati sevak Sangh, Nellore, 1971, Pg.: 135.
5. Ibid. Pg.: 135.
6. Ibid. Pg.: 135.

Chapter : Fourteen

Tana Bhagat Movement

(So long as we (Oraons) will keep on selling our labour, we will remain poor) .

Tana Bhagat Andolan (Movement)

The religion of the Oraons and prior to entry into Chhotanagpur, their society was of a high level. But with their entry into Chhotanagpur, their deterioration started gradually due to the important role played by the Munda society. The import of spirits and ghosts in Kudukh religion was from Munda religious system.[1] The Oraon did not know ghosts and spirits nor the rituals for their worship. Hence, when the Mundas were vacating their homes and lands for the Oraons and going away, then some Mundas who were knowledgeable about the subject were asked to stay back so that from time to time offerings could be made to the ghosts and spirits to keep them satisfied and peaceful. Time passed. At one time it so happened that all the tribes of Chhotanagpur became totally pre-occupied by ghosts and spirits. Even for minor sorrowful incidents it used to be taken for granted that they were caused by spirits and ghosts. At that time Sokha, Mati, Ojha came into existence. Their work was to identify the ghosts and spirits and to satisfy and quieten them. For this, sacrifice of cocks or he-goats, wine and service charges in the form of money had to be given which was an expensive solution. In this context three things were clear-first, ghost was more powerful than Ojha, Mati and Sokha, therefore the three used to worship, pray and plead with the ghost. Second, the ghost could leave the affected person or it might not also; this depended upon its whim and fancy whether it accepted the worship and prayers or else it would not go also. Third, due to greed for receiving more offerings it could come back.

During this anti-religious time, the Bhagat community came into existence. The Bhagat addressed the primeval Oraon society as Madua Oraon meaning omnivorous, the Oraon who eats meat, fish, drinks hard liquor, takes drugs and other intoxicants, and is impure and easy going. The Bhagat used to have a life style which was plain, simple, pure and pious. In dreams Mahadev would give instructions and according to them after getting a Mahadev pind (lump of rock) used to set it up there within a Mahadev Kuti (hut) and offer fruits, flowers and sweets along with worship. The Bhagats used to meditate and offer devotion for hours together to Mahadev. People believed that due to intense devotion, the Bhagats could acquiue the powers of Mahadev. Whenever any patient visited a Bhagat for treatment then the Bhagat through some incantations and other rituals could identify the ghost. Thereafter coming into a rage he would order the ghost to leave the patient and would warn that if it came ever again then its arms and legs would be broken.[2]

In this way, with the coming of the Bhagats the entire equation and identification of the ghosts went hay wire. Instead of worship, offerings, prayers, there was now talk of driving away the ghosts. Fear of the dominance of the ghosts was waning. In such circumstances, the father of the Tana Bhagat movement Jatra Oraon was born in 1888 in Chingri Nawatoli of Bishunpur block of the now Gumla district. His father was Kohra Bhagat. It is said that Jatra Oraon was born on 2 October, the birth day of Gandhiji, and even now a mela is held in his birthplace on his birth day. The starting years of Jatra's life were spent in his village. He was sober and quiet by nature right from childhood. By being influenced by his nature, his father thought of making him an ojha. A little distance away from the village was Hessag village, home to well known Ojha Turiya Bhagat. It was here that Jatra was sent to acquire learning of an Ojha. Jatra started getting trained with full dedication. He also was gathering knowledge regarding various roots and herbs. But in his mind a question used to arise that if the ghost has the patient in his captivity then how can the sacrifice of a cock release the patient from the ghost's captivity ? Hopeful of getting a cock, the ghost will dig deep into the patient and hold on to him with greater force. It is better therefore that just like the devotee of "Bhuifoot Mahadev," instead of worshipping and praying to the ghosts they should be driven out.

Jatra in his life had seen the atrocities committed by the zamindar and contractor on the Oraons. He had also seen the exploitation by the money-lenders, the Oraon's poverty, the increasing wrath of the ghosts. He was worried as to how and in what manner the economic condition of the Oraon society could be improved. Gradually, in his youth the thought began to firm up that so long as the Oraon will keep on moving here and there their condition will worsen continuously. The Oraon have only one God, Dharmesh, and fully concentrated devotion to Him can reform the lives of the oraons. This was the formative period of the life of Jatra.

One night, when Jatra was returning after his training hours, Dharmesh appeared before him and advised him to leave the training of Ojha-Mati because along with killing of animals ghosts are also worshipped.[3] In Kudukh religion killing any kind of creature is prohibited. Dharmesh directed Jatra to make the people aware of the directions of God and to show them the correct path. After saying this, Dharmesh disappeared from sight.

Such was this incident that it did not take long to spread. From next morning, visitors started crowding to his house. Whoever heard about it immediately started for Jatra's house. Jatra said that God was like a mass of light. He told them about the following directions of God Dharmesh :

(i) The Oraon should lead simple and pure life-this will ensure God's grace in him.

(ii) Killing of any kind of creature is prohibited. When we cannot give life then we have no right to take away life. We should not eat meat.

(iii) Every morning we should take our bath first and thereafter worship God . Prior to worship, intake of food is prohibited.

(iv) No intoxicants, wine, hadiya should be taken and no meal should be taken with a person taking such drinks/ intoxicants.

(v) Dancing and singing is prohibited in "Dhumkuriya," "akhra" or anywhere else because in a simple life there is no place for singing and dancing.

(vi) Hunting is prohibited.

(vii) Killing or torturing animals is a sin especially to make bullockspull the plough or carts. The Tana Bhagats replaced bullocks with buffaloes.

Jatra had given some instructions in the name of God which in a special way proved to be helpful in the development of a pure society. In addition to these rules, Jatra had emphasized on one rule that apart from his own race, Oraon would not sell his labour to others. So long as Oraon would benefit others through his labour, he would not be free from poverty.

Apparently it looked like an ordinary rule that when labour was of the Oraon, why should there be compulsion whether he should work or not. But in later years, this rule acquired a serious form. The aim of this movement was that the Oraon should rise above the present fallen social, economic, and religious condition and try to regain the heights of social and religious life of his Kudukh ancestors. The ardent desire to rise above was very powerful in the mind of the Oraon hence in a very short time the movement became quite successful. It is said that at that time the total number of Tana Bhagats in Ranchi, Palamau and Hazaribagh was 2,60,000.[4]

In the hymns and prayers of the Tana Bhagats, the work "Tana" was used frequently. The meaning of "Tana" "is to pull up." Catch hold of the ghosts, pull them out and drive them away. Pull up the society and religion and reach them to a higher level. The village from where the ghosts were driven out, the people of that village would gather at midnight on the outside limits of the village at an ident ified place. They would stand in a semi circle and sing hymns to Dharmesh, sun, moon and other gods and goddesses. Suddenly, out of these villagers, one person would acquire a certain posture to indicate as if the village ghost is upon him. Meaning, the village ghost has left the village and now has come upon that person. Then again suddenly that person leaves the other villagers and stands apart at a short distance. The hymn singing becomes louder, the crowd becomes quite excited. The villagers thereafter started stamping their feet on the ground and shout in unison "Ghost, get out, get out" and start running after the imaginary ghost till the opposite limits of the village and drive it out. At the end, the village mahto lets go a he-goat a little away from the outside limit of the village in a different direction.[5] It is taken for granted that the village has been freed of ghosts and spirits. This midnight ritual of driving away ghost used to frighten and terrorize the zamindars and money-lenders. When the crowd used to come close then the zamindar used to go upstairs in the castle and hide.[6] The money–lenders also were in this plight. Complaints regarding this midnight activity reached the British officers. A daroga was appointed to enquire into the matter. The daroga witnessed such an incident of drawing out of ghost but he could not understand anything except that such midnight arrangement could be dangerous also. Hence, through Govt. order this arrangement was stopped.

Due to this interference, the dis-satisfaction among the Oraons against the British started spreading. The more Jatra Bhagat was becoming popular among his followers, the more intolerable he was becoming to the administration, zamindars and money-lenders. Due to the rule of not selling his labour by the Oraon for the work of other communities, all economic activities were breaking down. Influenced by the opinions of Jatra, the Oraons had decided not to work for other races. Some Oraons who had bullocks which could have been used to transport goods, were not made available for the same.[7] Zamindars and moneylenders were looking at their barren fields helplessly. The zamindars had never thought about such a situation. They began complaining to the govt. authorities. In the meantime, the First World War took place. There used to be discussion about the victory of the Germans. Bengal was very much influenced by it. Hence, the illiterate, uneducated yet religiously enthusiastic Tana Bhagats came to believe the German not as a country but as an unknown powerful god[8] who would drive away the British and free them. Thus, in some places, German baba / god came to be invoked through prayers.

Due to all these reasons, Jatra Bhagat came to be disliked by the Govt. but there was no solid reason for arresting Jatra under the law. Jatra's movement and policy were totally non-violent. At that time contractual work used to be received by Govt. authorities and Christian missionaries. A school building was being constructed in Dokotoli which was near Jatra Bhagat's village. More than half the work had been completed when the Oraons stopped working.[9] The contractors concerned with the constructing of the school building started petitioning the Govt. authorities. Ultimately it was decided to arrest Jatra Bhagat. The local police came and arrested Jatra Bhagat and seven of his followers. He was presented in the court of the subdivisional Magistrate, Gumla, where, after being charged for inciting his race and causing riotous situation he was sentenced to one and a half years of rigorous imprisonment.[10] When he came out of jail after completing his punishment, Jatra was suffering from physical breakdown. Jatra could not revive and very soon he died.[11] It is said that the zamindars and moneylenders who suffered due to Jatra, caused a lot of torture to him in jail.

Jatra's sacrifice did not go in vain. Although the main role of Jatra Bhagat had been to organize the Tana Bhagat movement yet thereafter, instead of being individual based, it took up the appearance of organisation based. The non-cooperation movement started by Jatra Bhagat was another big step. Jatra had told his followers that when their ancestors have bequeathed to them this land, gardens and groves, fields and farms, then why should they give rent to the British govt. hence do not give rent. This dictum spread like wild fire and the Tana Bhagats stopped paying rent. In order to collect arrears of rent, thousands of acres of land belonging to the Tana Bhagats were auctioned off but such strength had come to this movement that due to the efforts of the local mentors this movement continued. It was hard to stop it.[12] The Tana Bhagats had found their life style and ideals akin to Gandhiji's life style and ideals. Ultimately, they received Gandhiji's patronage in their nonviolent movement against the

British regarding not paying of rent. Due to this they received national recognition. The Deputy Commissioner Ranchi in his letter to the Commissioner had expressed his anxiety on the subject of increasing strength of the Tana Bhagats.[13] In 1931 when Gandhiji started his Civil Disobedience movement, then the Tana Bhagats had under the leadership of Siddhu Bhagat of Kudu thana, participated for the first time in this freedom movement. The Tana Bhagats also participated in the Gaya and Ramgarh sessions organized by the Congress.[14] Gandhiji used to think the Tana Bhagats his most dear followers. In the end, when India became independent, the Govt. of India waived the land rent of the Tana Bhagats but the Tana Bhagats are still waiting for the return of their auctioned lands as had been promised by Gandhiji.

In Sept. 2014 when Rahul Gandhi came to Ranchi, then the innocent Tana Bhagats met him and tried to remind him of his promise to return their lands which had been anctioned during British rule. Actually and truly, the movement is still on.

List of Reference Books

1. Roy, S. C. "Oraon Religion and Custom". Gyan Publishing House, Delhi, 1999, Pg. : 341.
2. Ibid.- Pg.: 307.
3. Ibid.- Pg.: 341.
4. Kumar, N.- "Bihar District Gazetteer, Ranchi," Revenue Deptt., Secretariat Press, Govt. of Bihar, Patna, 1970, Pg.: 73.
5. Roy, S. C. – O.R.C. Pg.: 351
6. Ibid. – Pg.: 344
7. Kumar, N. – R. G. Pg.: 74
8. Dhan O. Rekha – T. R. I. bulletin, July 1960, Pg.: 253
9. Roy, S. C. – Pg.: 342
10. Kumar, N. – R. G. Pg.: 71
11. Kumar, N. – R. G. Pg.: 73
12. (a) Dhan O. Rekha – Op. cit. Pg.: 160
    (b) B. Virottam – "Jharkhand : Itihas evam Sanskriti," Bihar Hindi Granth Academy, Patna 2006 Pg.: 352
13. Deputy Commissioner, Ranchi to Commissioner of Chhotanagpur, 9 March 1921, K. K. Datta : Freedom Movement in Bihar, Vol. I, 1857, Pg.: 338.
14. (a) Dhan O. Rekha – op.cit., Pg.: 160
    (c) B. Virottam – op.cit., Pg.: 352.

Chapter : Fifteen

"Duka Ho" 1931 Haribaba Movement

(Duka Ho of Kolhan threaded the Ho and Santhal tribes in one strand and gave birth to such an organization which went along with the independence movement and got assimilated in it) .

With the British stepping into Jharkhand, a tradition of revolt started which lasted till independence in some form or the other. Of the several reasons of revolt, the main was the cultivable land prepared by the ancestors which was connected to their economic condition as well as their religious beliefs, and due to the reason of economic greed of the British Govt. the exploitation by the moneylenders and zamindars continued which used to hurt their feelings. Gandhiji came here in 1925 and was very much influenced by the followers of Birsa and Tana Bhagat. One class of Munda and Oraon tribes joined the non-cooperation movement.[1] In one ashram 400 persons started spinning on the "charkha' i.e. the spinning wheel.[2] Now among the tribals the message of boycotting of taxes and the advent of Gandhiji's rule floated around.

In October-November 1930, a Santhal called Silu also known as Tara Chand declared himself in Rajabasa (Dalbhum) as a blessed healer and claimed that he had divine powers. He advised people to abstain from drinking.[3] He said that God has created the earth, no king has done it. Hence question does not arise that land revenue/tax be paid to the zamindar or govt.[4] On 13 May 1931 a huge crowd gathered at Rajabasa and in the excitement of freedom pulled down the telephone wires.[5] They also threatened the local authorities that they did not care for the British soldiers because they had a huge ununiformed army which could not be harmed at all by the British guns and with the help of that army they would surely gain independence.[6] One morning Tarachand was arrested. He had admitted the arrangement of pulling down the telephone wires.

Amidst these activities, a new sect arose in Dalbhum whose patron was Seraikela resident Duka Ho[7] who later on became very popular by the name of Haribaba. He built an "ashram" (hermitage) in the forest of Jamtigarha near Chitpil, 12 miles away on the north-west of Chakradhapur. Very soon, crowds started gathering to receive his blessings and to conduct worship (Puja).[8] He stressed on traditional purity and concentration. Major portion of his disciples consisted of "Ho" tribals. Haribaba told his followers to keep away from witch craft and decided to destroy the witches. For this he gave special blessing to the village priests and the Manki and Munda due to which his influence spread. Wherever the Manki and Munda were strong and influential, they remained disinterested in the Haribaba movement but wherever the Manki / Munda were young and ineffectual, they joined this movement to increase their strength and influence.[9]

At that time the main centre of the Congress was Chakradhapur. Haribaba had gone to the Congress headquarter on 19 July 1931 but he did not want to preach about non payment of land rent and neither had he donned Khadi clothes. But he thought it would be better to further his connectivity with Jaichand, the disciple of Tarachand. Jaichand made Hurangiya, about 7 miles away from Kharsawan, his place of abode. This place is situated at the base of a high hill near Tamar of Ranchi district. Both representatives used to discuss with each other and both were popular among the Hos and Santhals respectively. Tarachand started a very speedy publicity campaign for Haribaba. Haribaba declared that if the Hos followed his instructions they would experience ethereal and wonderful happiness. The procedure to enter this sect was very difficult. The applicant would have to leave his village and stay in the sacred Sarna place alongwith his wife and children for a week. They would have to live on only one meal a day. After seven days the priest of the Haribaba sect would come to them alongwith some other representatives and material for worship and after adding some rituals he would proclaim their inclusion in the sect. Haribaba gave some instructions which were as follows :

(1) Singbonga is the highest God.
(2) Every day one must take a bath and the women must bathe twice a day, in the morning and evening.
(3) Sacred thread should be put on.
(4) Meat and fish should not be eaten.
(5) Liquor should not be imbibed.
(6) Thursday is a day of rest for sect members including their animals.

(7) Pigs are dirty, cocks and hens contaminate and dirty the food of the house, and black goat is the home of evil spirits-they should all be destroyed.

But there was difference of opinion among the Hos and Santhals. Universal religion and organization could have helped to tie them with one thread.[10] After release from jail on bail Tarachand straightaway reached the bordering area of Kharsawan. He got together about 4000 Kol, Bhumij and Santhal from Seraikela, Kharsawan and Tamar area and cutting down a huge tree alongwith other trees in the Raj protected Forest at Hurangada, he exhorted them to build a temple and houses. Thousands of trees were cut down. This activity without the Govt.'s permission proved intolerable for the administration. On 25 July the police reached Sini to arrest Tarachand. But by that time three to four thousand supporters reached there. They insulted the police and drove them away. The forlorn police returned to Kharsawan empthanded.[11] On 27 July Jaichand and his eleven supporters were arrested. The same day Duka Ho was caught in front of 300 persons but he remained courteous. Jaichand was charged for having misbehaved with the police and Duka was charged for a bad start to searching for witches, torturing butterflies and disrupting peace in the area. This public movement was quashed before it could change into a political movement. Hence action against these leaders was closed in 1931.[12]

The political side of this movement faded away but the religious feeling became very strong. The disciples of Haribaba admitted that he was fighting against the British.[13] After his release from jail, Haribaba disappeared. His statue was built. Waist downloads his body was of stone but abovethe waist he looked as if made of flesh and blood. His head had 2 braids of hair from which milk flowed out of one and water flowed out of the other. Both plaits had strange strength and represented good health and wealth.[14] Haribaba's disciples gave the picture of a religious organisation to this movement. In order to conduct an organization, money is required. Hence the activity regarding exorcism of ghosts and spirits took on a virulent form. Taking recourse to continuous sounding of the "nagara" and "gonga," his disciples would enthusiastically sing and dance and create a hullabaloo to reach the Sarna place and try to drive away the spirits from every nook and corner. Also, they would chant inter mittently "Hari bole," "Hari Baba ki jai" and "Gandhiji Ki Jai". In whatever thing an evil spirit was supposed to be lurking, it used to be thrown away. The mud stoves and the old cooking versels at home used to be broken up. The thatched roofs would be shaken to see if spirits were not hiding there. They declared that all those people who would remain away from that movement will have to suffer the curse of Haribaba. It was made compulsory to use milk, fruits, "Sirini" and camphor and incense for worship. After slight alterations, the highest God of the Mundas i.e. Singhbonga, and traditional prayers were adopted in the movement.[15] In the place of Adivasi dance, a new mixed kind of dance took over.

The authorities of Singhbhum decided to take stern steps. The Haribaba movement was declared to be illegal. The Mankis and Mundas were asked to close this movement. The Deputy Commissioner toured the villages which had adopted this new religion. He broke down the bamboo enclosures and huts which were used to keep materials related to ghosts and spirits, old musical instruments, dead rats and house-lizards in the belief that within those materials the ghosts have been captured. The authorities of Ranchi and Patna used to think that due to that movement political encouragement was spreading. The Christian missionaries also used to tell them various kinds of stories about them. They suspected the Manki and Munda that they could turn the movement against them. Although, the Singhbhum officer were thought to have over-reacted, yet they admitted their success as correct.

Still then, this movement area spread from Tamar, Khunti, Ranchi to the Oraon area of Gumla, Simdega to Odisha's Gangpur. Women took major part in this movement, hence many Harima came up. Haribaba's young wife Nanikai who used to propagate Haribaba's religion was called Hari-Ma. She constructed an "akhra" at Mandpur near Manoharpur, and started distributing "Hari Pani" on payment basis. Whoever used to come to her, she would take a written agreement from him that he would not disturb the property of anybody and would not disobey the orders of the Govt.[16] Near Palkot, Hari-Mai appeared dressed in tiger skin. Hari-Mai of Gumla got a bond executed that if they left the religion then Govt. would punish them. In some places it became a matter of earning money, too.

But it could never put on the hue of a political movement and the movement never joined the Congress in any manner.[17] The Christian Missionaries felt highly irritated by this movement and saw it as a danger to their own existence. Many converted Christians returned to the Haribaba sect. In Ranchi there was a scuffle between the Roman Catholic and this new religion.[18] The Christians charged its rival with giving a bad name to their religion, of having destroyed the purity of their worship place and breaking down their mud stoves and pitchers. A case was also filed in a court but the Christians lost the case.[19]

This movement was the only way towards a reformist movement. In those days there was financial depression and politics was facing an atmosphere of troublous times. Due to suspicion of evil spirits, the selling price of goats and chicken fell, leading to loss for the adivasis and financial difficulties. The price of mud pitchers rose. For a few years Hari Baba's movement went on effectively and enthusiastically. The Christian Missionaries alleged that the ancient Munda religion was being destroyed and lower level Hinduism was being adopted. The Sarna adivasis were terrified that the people of the Hari Baba sect were destroying the purity of their sacred Sarna place due to which the village god in anger would bring in starvation. Hence they decided that anyhow the sanctity of the Sarna place would be maintained and they did that.[20] The British govt. feared that the Ho who were loyal to the simple sect may not instigate their cunning and intelligent disciples against the British which would result in an impediment to the strength of the administration and its steadiness.[21] This movement spread in Ranchi district after growing and becoming large among Hos, Mundas and Oraons. The sadans also joined this movement. The Rule of Gandhi is coming, the British are going, stop giving tax, etc. were the slogans being shouted. The British were afraid that the driving out of ghosts and spirits would mean, sooner or later, the authorities and foreigners which could have been dangerous and violence could erupt, revolt may take place. But this did not happen and with the progress of struggle for independence this movement slackened.

This movement, in some ways, was like a cultural movement. Just like Birsa and Tana Bhagat movements, this movement also brought in some reforms and drove out socially evil practices. The participation of women in this movement was more. This was the expression of some years of anger in the adivasi world which got strengthened with the advent of Gandhiji.

List of Reference Books

1. Kumar Suresh Singh, Dust-storm and Hanging Mist, story of Birsa Munda and his movement, Firms, 1965.
2. Quoted in Dutta, K. K., History of the freedom movement in Bihar, Vol. 1, Pg.: 473-6.
3. A. Majid to A. D. Tuckey, Commissioner Chhotanagpur, dated Hazaribagh the 27th March 1931, Political special Deptt., Pg.: 12-13.
4. Ward to Tuckey, Chaibasa, 30th July 1931, Pg.: 33-38, c. Ibid.
5. Extract from confidential diary of the Superintendent of Police, Manbhum, dated 8th March, Pg.: 9, c. Ibid.

6. Extract from Confidential diary of Superintendent of Police, Singhbhum, Ibid; Pg.: 20, for the period ending 27 May 1931, Ibid, Pg. : 20-21.
7. Extract from confidential diary of Superintendent of police, Santhal Parganas, dated Dumka 9 June 1931, Pg.: 23, Ibid.
8. Ward to Tuckey, 127 C, July 28, 1931
9. Dikson, Rev. G. W., Extract from Singhbhum Confidential Diary for the week ending 15 Jan. 1932.
10. Extract from A. D. Tuckey's fortnightly D. O. No. 287 T.C., dated 27 July 1931, Ibid. Pg.: 28.
11. Sriram Chandra Singh Deo Raj, Ruling Chief of the Kharsawan state to D. C. Singhbhum, dated Kharsawan 26 July 1931.
12. Ward to Tuckey, Chaibasa 28 and 30 July, 1931.
13. Dickson, G. W. "The Hari Baba Movement, what it is," Chhotanagpur Diocesan Paper no. : 40 (New Series).
14. Vanhoutte, G. "Hari Baba". Chhotanagpur Mission letter no: 11, Nov. 1931, Pg.: 236-39.
15. O Haribaba, you are our Father and mother rising like milk and setting like curd. Save us in sickness and troubles. Let our land remain happy. Drive away the condition. Let us realize true wisdom henceforth.
16. Extracts from confidential diary of Superintendent of Police, Singhbhum dated 8th October 1931, Chief Secretary's special section, Pg.: 45.
17. A. D. Tuckey, Commissioner of Chhotanagpur to P. C. Tallents, Chief Secretary to Govt. of Bihar and Orissa, D. O. no. : 277 TC dated 16 May, 1932.
18. See for example, Ranchi S. R. case no.: 52 of 1932 Report no.: 1 dated 15.32. Extract from the Confidential Diary of the Superintendent of Police, Ranchi dated 1 May 1932.
19. Judgement Etwa Oraon Vrs. Chota Paulus Oraon, 12 June 1932.
20. Ibid, April, 1933 Chhotanagpur Diocesan Papers, Pg.: 5.
21. Dikson G. W. Extract from Singhbhum from Singhbhum Confident ial Diary for week of ending 15 Jan. 1932.

Chapter : Sixteen

In the name of unknown Martyrs

In the name of unknown martyrs

This chapter is dedicated to the name of unknown martyrs. The unknown martyrs are in-numerable in number and their cooperation is limitless. Unknown martyrs are mostly victims of group killings. The freedom struggle of 1857[1] is an example. The British Govt. had formulated Act. XVII, 1857 and made the punishments of hanging have a wider scope, easy and liberal, and implemented it. Simpson, the Deputy Commissioner of Hazaribagh, used this power freely.

The free soldiers were going from Doranda Cantonment to join the army of Thakur Kunwar Singh at Shahabad. They reached Chatra. The traders of Chatra did not give them rations, they did not cooperate. They were hungry for two days when Major English reached there with European and Sikh army. In the morning of 2 October, the British army attacked them. The free soldiers got defeated. Next day, 77 dead bodies were found on the battle field. A ditch was dug and those martyrs of freedom struggle were buried in it.

Raja Shambhu Nath Singh of Hazaribagh was loyal to the British. He was helping Simpson alongwith his army. Some of the wounded soldiers had been successful in running away toward the forest. The Hazaribagh soldiers brought the wounded soliders of Doranda and presented them to Simpson who got them hanged. After that the bodies would be thrown in a nearby take. The Hazaribagh sepoys would be given five rupees per head and they would catch hold of the injured soldiers hiding in the forest for whom the hangman's noose would always be ready. The lake, well known as "fansi talab" or "lake of hangings" has so many stories within it that no body knows about them.

In this context mention may be made of Kumar Suresh Singh[2] when the army had done firing on the hill of Sayeel-Rakab and in which Mundas fighting for Munda Raj got killed and to show reduced number of dead Mundas or for any other reason, the martyrs were buried. Jharkhand's unknown martyrs would not be few in number. What is required is to identify them.

Jharkhand is such a tribal land on which revolt started with the British putting their foot on it. On a lower level or a bigger level, the slogan "our country, our Rule" echoed throughout the rivers-hills-forests to the vast plains and made them tremble. Behind this echo was the strength of the sacrifice of thousands of unknown martyrs who are still unidentified. The country pays homage to them on Martyr's Day. The independence of the country is aware that its freedom is the fruit of the sacrifice of these unknown martyrs.

List of Reference Books

1. Act XVII of 1857
2. Dr. K. Suresh Singh, Birsa Munda and His Movement, News Delhi, 1979 Pg.:

Epilogue

The martyrs of Jharkhand were chiefly the fruits of tribal revolt, 1857 of the war of independence and various movements. These martyrs led the tribals for home rule against the British. The British administrative machinery, historians and news-magazines described these revolts to be uprisings against the zamindars (land lords), contractors and money-lenders but never against the British Govt. This kind of publicity was to show the clean image of the British Govt. as also to develop hatred and disgust among the tribals against the Hindus Both communities had lived together for ages but the aim was to divide them. W. W. Hunter had used the word "Hindu" to denote zamindar, moneylender, and bania etc. In his book "Annals of Rural Bengal." This kind of usage reveals the distorted British mentality.

The exploitation by contractors, zamindars and money-lenders cannot be totally denied but it was not the main reason. The root cause of tribal revolt was the Regulation system of the British administration. The law framed for the plains of Bengal-Bihar was, without applying any mind, made applicable to the tribal areas, too. The tribes which had traditionally lived under the administrative arrangement of Munda-Manki, Patti-Parha home-rule, could not tolerate British administration so they rose up in arms against it. This revolt in a limited way was a freedom-fight against the British Govt. for which many brave men/women sacrificed their lives and came to be worshipped as martyrs. The martyrdom of Buddhu Bhagat and Siddhu-Kanhu are proof of it.

The British authorities thought about the reasons for such revolts in detail and the conclusion came out that the tribal areas should be kept within non-Regulation administrative system for the protection of their well-being.

As a result of these revolts, the tribals were freed from the regulation administration and their customs were given due importance and allowed to start again under a non-regulation administration. The South West Frontier Agency was started which was a vast tribal area with headquarters at Ranchi and including all nearby tribal areas. In addition to Chhotanagpur, Santhal

Pargana was created and in this the rights of the Santhals were protected under a non-Regulation administrative system. After the implementation of the non-Regulation administrative system. there was no tribal revolt although in this area the zamindars, money-lenders etc. remained settled.

The chief martyrs of the freedom struggle of 1857 were Thakur Vishwanath Shahdev, Pandey Ganpat Rai, and Tikait Umrao Singh. About 600 sepoys under the leadership of Thakur Vishwanath Shahdev had gone from Doranda Cantonment to Chatra from where they were supposed to move onward to join the army of Babu Kunwar Singh. In Chatra, the traders did not co-operate, rations could not be obtained and the sepoys were hungry for two days. In the meantime Major English reached Chatra with troops consisting mostly of Sikhs and attacked these freedom fighters. Some were killed, some were wounded and some escaped.

The next day, the battlefield was found strewn with 77 dead bodies which were interred in a locally dug ditch. The wounded and captured sepoys were presented before the District Magistrate Simpson of Hazaribagh, there was a brief hearing after which they were punished with death by hanging. Thereafter they were buried locally or else their bodies were thrown into a lake. Similar such unknown martyrs lie interred beneath the land.

Jharkhand saw 2 chief movements. Both movements had a special feature-they wanted to go for social reform, were worshippers of pure religion yet after some time they leaned more towards politics. The period of activity of Birsa Munda was in the last decade of the 19th century, and that of Jatra Oraon was the second decade of the 20th century. The British Govt. had arrested both propagators. It is said that Birsa was poisoned to death, and Jatra, upon the instigation of zamindars, was beaten up in jail to such an extent that very soon within a few months of being released from jail he passed away. After Jatra, the Tana Bhagat movement had spread far and wide among the Oraons. Birsa Munda is the most popular Martyr.

Jharkhand has given birth to brave warriors and has never been without martyrs. The martyrs who have been mentioned as well as those who could not be mentioned, those martyrs are also entitled for respect and reverence.

List of Books

1. Ambastha, G. P. : Bihar Darpan, Patna 1940.
2. Ahmad, J. : Bihar Ke Adivasi, Motilal Banarsidas, New Delhi, 1957.
3. Dutta, K. K. : Bihar me Angreji Raj Ke Virudh? Ashanti, Patna, 1975.
4. Minz, Diwakar : Munda and Oraon Ka Dharmik Itihas, Orient Publications, New Delhi, 1996.
5. Roy Choudhary, Pranav Chandra : Bihar me 1857 Chhotanagpur Tatha Santhal Pargana, Patna, 1959.
6. Sahay, Govind : Sun Beyalis Ka Vidroh, Indore, 1946
7. Singh, Kumar Suresh : Birsa Munda our unka Andolan, Vani Prakashan, Delhi, 2001.
8. Vidyarthi, Lalita Prasad : Bihar Ke Adivasi, Shukla Book Depot, Patna – 1988.
9. Trived, Da, Sa : Prang Maurya Bihar, Bihar Rashtra Bhasha Parishad, Patna, 1954.
10. Ahluwalia, M. M. : Freedom Struggle in India (1858-1900) Delhi, 1965.
11. Ambast, N. K. : A Critical Study of Tribes Education, S. Chand & Co., Delhi- 1970.
12. Birt, Bradey F. B. : (i) Chhotanagpur a little known Province of the Empire, London, 2nd Indian Edition, 1970.
    (ii) Story of an Indian upland, London, 1905.
13. Bompass, C. H. : Folk lore of Santhal Parganas, London 1909.
14. Campion, Edmund : My Oraon Culture, Catholic Press, Ranchi.

15. Choudhury, S. B. : Civil Disturbances under British Rule (1757-1955), Calcutta- 1955.

16. Dalton, E. T. : Descriptive Ethnology of Bengal, Calcutta 1872.

17. Dutta, K. K. : (i) The Santhal Insurrection, Secretariat Press, Calcutta.
(ii) Unrest against British Rule in Bihar 1831-1859, Patna, 1957.
(iii) History of Freedom movement in Bihar 2 vols., Patna 1957.

18. Desa, F. : Crisis in Chhotanagpur, Bangalore, 1957.

19. Dehon, P. : Religion and Customs of Oraons, Calcutta, 1905.

20. Diwakar, R. R. : Bihar through the Ages, Patna, 1958.

21. Elwin, V. H. : The Aboriginals, Bombar 1942

22. Evans, P. : Theories of Primitive Religion, Clarendon Press, Oxford-1865.

23. Griffith, W. G. : The Kol Tribes of Central India, The Royal Asiatic Society of Bengal, Calcutta 1956.

24. Hah, F. : Oraon Folk Lore, Govt. Press, Patna 1931.

25. Hoffman, J. B. : Encyclopaedia Mundarica, Govt. Press, Patna 1950-74.

26. Hunter, W. W. : (i) Annals of Rural Bengal, London 1868.
(ii) The statistical Account of Bengal, Vols. XVI-XVII, London, 1875.

27. Hutton, J. K. : Caste in India, Bombay, 1975.

28. Jha, J. C. : The Tribal Revolt of 1831-32, K. P. Jaiswal Research Institute, Patna- 1987.

29. Kumar, Purushottam : Mutinies and Rebellions in Chhotanagpur (1831-32) New Delhi, 1991.

30. Majumdar, R. C. : History of the Freedom Movement in India, Secretariat Press, Calcutta, 1962

31. Majumdar, D. N. : Races and Cultures in India, Lucknow 1944.

32. Man, E. G. : Santalia and the Santhals, Calcutta 1876.

33. Minz, N. (ed.) : Tribal Awakening, Madras, 1965.

34. Meulder, De S. T. : The India Mutiny Tribal India, Speak, Poona, 1952.

35. Milton, Richard : The Indian Mutiny, London, 1957.

36. Mirra, B. B. : Central Administration of the East India Company, Manchester, 1959.

37. Prasad, N. : Land and People of Tribal Bihar, TRI Ranchi 1961.

38. Ponette : The Munda World, Catholic Press, Ranchi, 1978

39. Rosner, Victor : The Flying Horse of Dharmes, Satya Shanti Publication, Ranchi 1982.

40. Raghavaiah, V. : Tribal Revolts, Andhra Rushtra Adimjati Sewak Sangh, Nellore-1971.

41. Risley, H. H. : The Tribes and Castes of Bengal, Secretariate Press, Calcutta, 1891.

42. Roy, S. C. : (i) The Mundas and their Country, Catholic Press, 2nd reprint 1995, Crown Publication, Ranchi.
(ii) The Oraons of Chhotanagpur, 2nd reprint Crown Publication, 1994, Ranchi.
(iii) Oraon Religion and Customs, 2nd reprint, 1999 Gyan Publishing House, Delhi.

43. Sinha, S. P. : (i) Santal-Hul, TRI, Ranchi 1991
(ii) Life and Times of Birsa Bhagwan, Patna, 1964

44. Singh, Kumar Suresh : (i) The Dust storm and Hanging Mist a study of Birsa Munda and his movement in Chhotanagpur (1874-1901) Calcutta, 1966.
(ii) Tribal Movement in India Manshar Publication, N. D. 1982.

45. Spry, H. H. : Modern India, 2 Vols. London 1837.

46. Vidyarthi, L. P. : The Maler, Bosland Pvt. Ltd. Calcutta 1963.

47. News papers and Periodicals : Ranchi Express, (Hindi Daily) Ranchi. 4 Jan. 1998. Ghar-Bandhu (Hindi Fortnightly) GEL Mission, Ranchi.

48. The Bengali (Editor, Surendra Nath Banerjee), English Daily Calcutta, April to June 1990 "Munda Tribal".

49. Calcutta Review – 1968

50. Bengali Hurkaru – Jan.-June 1832 Calcutta, District Gazetteers

51. Kumar, N. : Bihar District Gazetteer Ranchi, Review Deptt. Govt. of Bihar, Patna 1970.

52. Choudhary P. C. Roy : Bihar District Gazetteer Hazaribag Secretariat Press, Govt. of Bihar, Patna, 1957.

53. Choudhary P. C. Roy : Bihar District Gazetteer Shahabad, Secretariat Press, Govt. of Bihar, Patna, 1961.

54. Choudhary P. C. Roy : Bihar District Gazetteer Dhanbad, Govt. of Bihar, Patna, 1966.

55. Choudhary P. C. Roy : Bihar District Gazetteer Singhbhum, Secretariat Press, Govt. of Bihar, Patna, 1964.

56. Malley, L.S.S.O. : Santhal Pargana, 2nd Reprint, Logos Press, New Delhi, 1999.

Index

S

T